Garden View Appliqué

Vintage Album Patterns

Faye Labanaris

American Quilter's Society
P. O. Box 3290 • Paducah, KY 42002-3290
www.AQSquilt.com

Located in Paducah, Kentucky, the American Quilter's Society (AQS) is dedicated to promoting the accomplishments of today's quilters. Through its publications and events, AQS strives to honor today's quiltmakers and their work and to inspire future creativity and innovation in quiltmaking.

Editor: Barbara Smith
Graphic Design: Lisa M. Clark
Cover Design: Michael Buckingham
Photography: Charles R. Lynch

Library of Congress Cataloging-in-Publication Data
Labanaris, Faye
  Garden view appliqué : vintage album patterns / by Faye Labanaris.
    p. cm.
   ISBN 1-57432-784-4
   1. Appliqué--Patterns.   2. Quilting--Patterns.   3. Album quilts.   4. Flowers
in art.   I. Title.
   TT779 .L255 2001
      746.46'041--dc21
                                        2001005808

Additional copies of this book may be ordered from the American Quilter's Society, PO Box 3290, Paducah, KY 42002-3290, or online at www.AQSquilt.com.

Copyright © 2001, Faye Labanaris

DEDICATION

This book is dedicated to…

THE ALBUM MAKERS OF LONG AGO,
whose work continues to inspire,
and blooms anew in the twenty-first century;

TO FRIENDS,
who stitched beautiful garden blocks;

TO FAMILY
whose love makes everything bloom beautifully.

TULIPS I

Stitched by Elizabeth Devlin, Falmouth, MA. A bright floral fabric contrasts strongly with the dark green background. The tulips are mounted on the straight of the grain, resulting in a diamond-shaped center. Pattern 7.

OLD ENGLISH ROSE

Stitched by Berta Murray, University Park, MD. A gentle meadow of wild-flowers provides the color theme for the flowers in this block. Couched cord stems add texture. Pattern 27.

We have a little garden,
A garden of our own,
And every day we water there
The seeds that we have sown.

We love our little garden,
And tend it with such care,
You will not find a faded leaf
Or blighted blossom there.

—Anonymous
Cecily Parsley's Nursery Rhymes

WREATH BOUQUET

Flowers made by the author, block stitched by Rhonda Kleiman, Fords, NJ. The centers of the flowers are filled to overflowing with French knots in a variety of threads and beads. Making a real bow is easier than appliquéing one. Pattern 37.

This book is not the work of only one person. Many people worked behind the scenes to arrive at this final form. I would like to express my heartfelt thank you…

To the American Quilter's Society and publisher Meredith Schroeder for wanting to publish this, my third, book with them. I appreciate your support and patience with an unorthodox author.

To my editor Barbara Smith for being there each step of the way with the gift of a gentle listening ear, encouragement, and excitement with this endeavor. Her skills at editing make it easy to accept cuts and changes.

To Eugenia Barnes, thank you for listening with your heart and for being there from the conception of this project to its completion. Your insight and understanding of the work of our album ancestors and your encouragement of my attempt to bring these patterns into the twenty-first century helped me more than I can say.

ACKNOWLEDGMENTS

Won't you come into my garden?
I'd like my roses to see you.

Richard Brinsley Sheridan

To Ellen Peters, for helping me to stitch up a storm. Her skill at machine quilting turned many of these orphan blocks into beautiful garden quilts. I couldn't have quilted so many, so beautifully, in such a short period of time.

To the 85 initial "adventurers," members of the Cocheco Quilters Guild, Dover, New Hampshire; the Baltimore Appliqué Society, Baltimore, Maryland; and my students in an assortment of classes across the United States and in England for taking part in this new adventure in making an album quilt. Your enthusiasm and comments were encouraging.

To the 36 quiltmakers who continued on this adventure with me and provided many wonderful blocks for this book. Your personality shows in your work, and each block in this garden album book is filled with uniqueness and friendship. A very special thank you to all of you! This book would not have bloomed as beautifully without you.

To the fabric manufacturers and quilt shops who keep us inspired and stocked with so many wonderful fabrics. Just keep them coming!

To Mickey Lawler (SkyDyes), for hand painting truly wonderful fabrics that give a unique touch to many of these blocks.

To my husband, Nick, for giving me the love and the freedom to bloom in many ways and in many places. Home is best, and one's own garden is always the most beautiful.

CONTENTS

CALENDULA
Stitched by Lisa Louise Adams, Volcano, HI. A summer's day in a meadow filled with butterflies and wildflowers serves as the background for this beautiful bouquet. The flower centers are accented with beads. Pattern 25.

BLOOMING HEARTS II
Stitched by Elizabeth Devlin, Falmouth, MA. A springtime leafy green appliqué fabric is right at home in the poppies. Pattern 9.

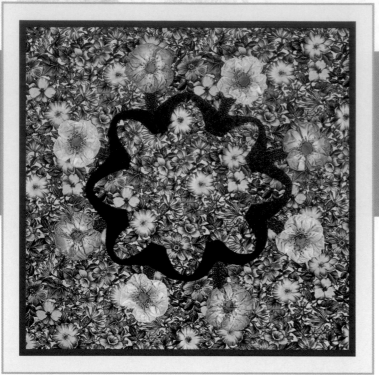

HYACINTHS

Flowers made by the author, block stitched by Ann McClain, Colorado Springs, CO. Ann has used five-petal ribbon roses with embroidered centers for her flowers and textured trim for her stems. This is a simple block with so many possibilities. Pattern 28.

*The greatest gift of the garden
is the restoration of the five senses.*

Hanna Rion

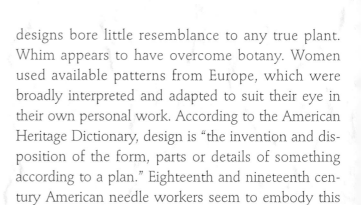

Patchwork allowed quiltmakers to work with scraps in a geometric format. Most often, the resulting items were considered household work, that is, functional bed quilts. Appliqué afforded these same needle women the opportunity to work with scraps in a different, more elaborate or decorative format. A great body of appliqué works still exist because many of these were "best" quilts. They therefore survived because they were not utilitarian as many piecework quilts were.

American needlework was greatly influence by Elizabethan designs, especially in the use of plant forms. Little attention was paid to the actual botanical structure of the plants in that many designs contained fruits and flowers not of the same species. It was the same with leaves and berries. In many cases, the designs bore little resemblance to any true plant. Whim appears to have overcome botany. Women used available patterns from Europe, which were broadly interpreted and adapted to suit their eye in their own personal work. According to the American Heritage Dictionary, design is "the invention and disposition of the form, parts or details of something according to a plan." Eighteenth and nineteenth century American needle workers seem to embody this definition with their appliqué appearing as variations, adaptations, and interpretations.

Eugenia Barnes
Marcellus, New York
AQS Certified Appraiser,
Teacher, Lecturer

PREFACE

I have enjoyed every minute working on this book. Mainly, it involved playing with fabrics, patterns, and ribbon. The actual writing was done in January with snow on the ground. I kept a small bouquet of fresh flowers on my desk, so I could keep glancing over at fresh floral beauty as I wrote about floral beauties in fabric. My life has changed a bit since this book was conceived almost two years ago. This floral adventure has affected my shopping habits, decorating preferences, and gardening techniques. I am richer for these changes.

From my journal, June 1999:

June is busting out all over! I have been in floral heaven since I left cold New Hampshire in early April. My travels took me first to Lancaster, Pennsylvania, with the first spring blooms of the year for me to enjoy, then on to California with lush tropical vegetation and flowers! Then to Paducah, Kentucky, with dogwood in bloom, then on to England in May. I could write pages about the English blooms, cottage gardens, climbing roses, the countryside. It was all so beautiful! I timed my return just right as spring time had arrived in New England. Many new purchases at garden centers and a planting session with my husband have given my garden a lush new look. (I've told him all these new plants and gardens are necessary inspiration for my quilts.)

I hope you enjoy this garden album adventure. May you take time to smell the flowers and enjoy the pleasure of gentle stitching.

Faye Labanaris

VINTAGE ROSE WREATH, ca. 1850

From the collection of the author. This delicate antique wreath block has stuffed-work leaves, roses, buds, and calyxes. There are many variations of roses and buds in it, so I think the maker interpreted the pattern as she stitched it.

*If you love flowers, fabric, and gardens,
then you are in store for a great floral adventure!
Lovingly first stitched and now re-stitched,
forty-five heirloom blocks bloom anew!*

Floral album blocks come alive in the twenty-first century with an exciting new look. Traditionally, a light-colored solid fabric was used for the background, with the appliqué cut from a darker solid color or a small-scale print. With so many wonderful fabrics continually coming on the market, including many reproductions and collections, now is your chance to create a garden album quilt of vintage blocks with a contemporary twist – the freedom to create unusual fabric combinations.

The idea grew from my love of Baltimore Album quilts. For the past 12 years, I have been interested in them. These stunningly complex beauties totally captivate me, and they are the main source of inspiration for my work. As we approached the millennium, I found myself drawn to the early album quilts made in the 1800s. The floral blocks made so long ago have an ageless appeal that continues to inspire. These quilts of the pre- and post-Baltimore Album quilt era have a simplicity and an elegance all their own. As I studied them, I started selecting favorite

blocks and soon came up with more than 100 I wanted to make. Realistically, I weeded that number down to 50. It was not an easy process with so many wonderful blocks to choose from.

This is a new adventure in making an album quilt. Put aside the traditional colors of green and red mounted on a muslin background. Select floral and foliage prints, mix and match with a sprinkling of hand-painted beauties, Bali batiks, and tone-on-tones for a garden fabric adventure that will delight the fabric lover in you.

Album blocks of wreaths and paper-cut designs take on a whole new appearance when using chintz and large-scale florals as inspirational fabrics for appliqué foregrounds as well as backgrounds. Stitch up one block or more, pick as many as you like. The fabric's design makes it easier than you might think.

We'll combine these floral blocks in a garden setting, much like planning and planting a living garden. We are going for a floral look, varying from sparse to lush. It will be a busy-looking quilt, but so is a lush cottage garden. Everywhere you look there is beautiful color. Upon close inspection, you see and appreciate the individual blocks and their embellished details.

Just have fun making these blocks, and the resulting quilts will burst into bloom before you know it. Think of this book as a garden catalog, a starting point for planning your own garden quilt.

GETTING STARTED

OREGON ROSE

Stitched by the author. Traditional Album colors appliquéd on a hand-painted fabric background give this block a feel of tradition with a contemporary twist. Pattern 26.

The most noteworthy thing about gardeners is that they are always optimistic, Always enterprising, and never satisfied. They always look forward to doing better than they have ever done before.

Vita Sackville-West

"WREATH OF BUDS"

Stitched by the author. This classic wreath reminds me of crocuses in springtime. After a long cold winter in New England, I yearn for bright blue skies and beautiful, colorful crocuses. Pattern 29.

FABRIC LOVERS REJOICE!

This is an opportunity to use as many florals and foliage fabrics as you like, and you can't have too many flowers in your garden or fabrics in your collection. It takes time to discover a lush garden's individual components.

With 45 patterns to choose from, you are probably wondering just where to begin. Begin with fabric. Gather fabrics for consideration from your collection. Pull out those that speak to you, including floral prints of all scales from large to small, and a large assortment of greens.

Sort your fabrics

Sort selected fabrics into piles of greens, light soft florals, dark background florals, bright florals, and large-scale prints. Sorting will give you a feel for your fabric choices and the possible combinations. It will also enable you to shop better for any missing fabrics.

Playing with fabrics has a soothing effect. Shopping for fabrics has an exciting effect. Sharing fabrics has a warming effect.

You can never have too many greens in your collection. Variety in shades, prints, and textures all add a richness to the garden. Look for solids, subtle tie-dyes, Bali batiks, small prints with black or colored designs, foliage prints, and greens with small-scale blooms. Try various textures, such as cotton, ultra-suede, corduroy, velvet, tapestry, and wool.

The important thing is to gather fabrics you like. First sort by the scale of the print, then sort by background color into piles of light, medium, and dark fabrics. Keep greens separate. Also make a separate pile of landscape prints to use for ground, bricks, stones, and water.

The background fabric can be a floral print of large- to medium-scale or a green fabric, such as a hand-painted, hand-dyed, or batiked beauty. You could also use a tone-on-tone or a subtle foliage print.

The appliqué pieces can be a floral or green on a floral background, which can be either light or dark for contrast. In some cases, the background fabric and the appliqué may appear as one unit. It is only on close inspection that the appliqué work can be identified.

I have found that the large-scale decorator chintz fabrics really work beautifully. To retain the glazed appearance, I did not pre-wash my chintz; however, you can soak your fabrics in cool water, if you like.

Pair fabrics and patterns

You can start by pairing background and appliqué fabrics, in combinations such as a floral with a green or a light floral with a dark floral. When in doubt, work with green as one of the fabrics, it's a natural match. If some completed blocks lack contrast, add green either as appliquéd leaves or as an embroidered edge to outline the leaves. This outline appliqué technique defines and accents the pattern beautifully.

After pairing the fabrics, select the patterns you want to make. Trace the patterns on freezer paper and cut them out, ready to go. Once you have a pile of patterns and a pile of fabrics, you can begin combining the fabrics with the patterns. Concentrate on each block individually and don't worry about what the final quilt might look like. Just keep making blocks you like, one at a time.

If you pick one flower at a time, eventually you will have a bouquet!

*He who would have beautiful roses
in his garden must have
beautiful roses in his heart.*

Dean Hole

CHOOSE A TECHNIQUE

Use your favorite appliqué method or consider the following possibilities: For hand appliqué, you can needle-turn to a marked fold line or free needle-turn a motif. With machine appliqué, you can add beautiful decorative threads and fancy stitches.

Fused appliqué provides a quick method for making intricate designs, and there are many fusible products available in quilt shops. After fusing the appliqué pieces to the background, use either a hand or machine buttonhole-stitch embellishment to cover the raw edges. You can use both hand and machine appliqué in the same project.

Some of the block patterns lend themselves to decorative machine stitches, and more detail is better than less for these garden blocks. Tiny stems can be appliquéd, embroidered, or couched with decorative trim or cording. The fabric you use will partially determine what kind of embellishments to add. Let the fabrics speak to you.

If I'm not sure what to add for floral details, a fresh look at the blocks at a later time sometimes helps me.

Needle-turn appliqué

See Figure 1 for step-by-step instructions for the needle-turn technique. Use a thread color to match your appliqué fabric or a neutral, such as gray. Whether you are needle-turning to a marked line or free needle-turning a shape, turn under the edge for a distance of about ⅛". Take only two or three stitches at a time before turning under the next ⅛". Sewing in such small increments makes the process quite manageable. You can get in trouble if you try to turn under too much fabric at one time because it will be difficult to hold down. Just turn under enough to hold under your thumb.

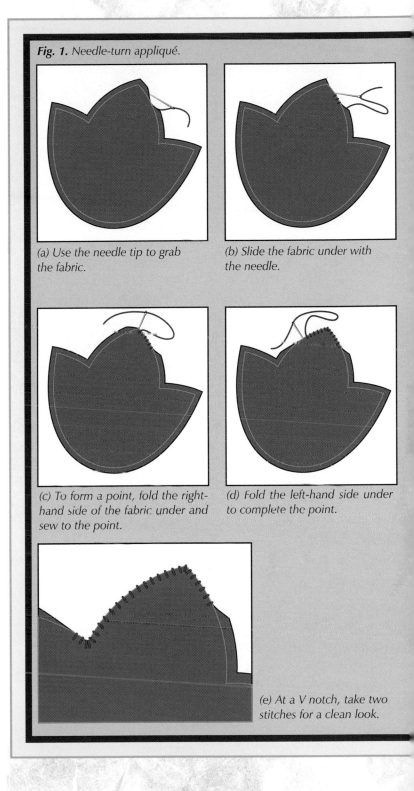

Fig. 1. *Needle-turn appliqué.*

(a) *Use the needle tip to grab the fabric.*

(b) *Slide the fabric under with the needle.*

(c) *To form a point, fold the right-hand side of the fabric under and sew to the point.*

(d) *Fold the left-hand side under to complete the point.*

(e) *At a V notch, take two stitches for a clean look.*

TIPS: To determine how much turn-under allowance you need to leave, try cutting and sewing only 2" along the appliqué edge at a time. Start with a ¼" allowance, and with each cut, make the allowance a little narrower. You'll soon know the right width for you.

Here is a good way to start needle-turning if you are new at it. Press a freezer-paper template, shiny side down, on the front of the appliqué fabric. Leave a scant ¼" turn-under allowance beyond the template as you cut out the fabric piece. There's no need to measure the allowance. Just cut it by eye. Pin or baste the fabric piece to the background. Needle-turn by using the freezer-paper's edge as a guide. If you like, you can move on to needle-turning on a marked line instead of using a freezer-paper guide.

Depending on the fabric, I use a fine-point permanent fabric pen to mark the turn line. Mark lightly. The line needs to be just dark enough to see, and it will disappear with the turn-under allowance.

On certain fabrics where a black or brown line does not show, I have used a fine gold pen. This color is especially useful if the background fabric is a metallic print.

Raw-edge. Place the template, right side up, on the front of the fabric and draw around it with a fine-point pen. Cut the fabric piece out on the line. Leaving the raw edges unturned, baste the appliqué piece to the background. If you prefer, you can stabilize the appliqué fabric first with fusible web before cutting it. If the piece has not been stabilized, the buttonhole stitches used to cover the raw edges will need to be closer together to prevent fraying.

There are several types of threads and buttonhole stitches you can use (Figure 2). Cotton or silk embroidery floss is a good thread choice. Select either a contrasting or matching thread color and use one or more strands. Be sure to try a few sample stitches to see if you like the results.

Ultrasuede. Ultrasuede is the easiest of all fabrics to hand appliqué. It is a wonderful time saver, especially when used for something as intricate as rose calyxes. Mark the wrong (smooth) side of the ultrasuede with an "X" so you will know which side is the front (the fuzzier side).

Make a template from the pattern and mark its front side. Turn the template over and place it on the marked side of the ultrasuede (marked sides together). Trace around the template with a fine-point marking pen. Cut the appliqué piece just barely outside the marked line. Position the piece where desired on the background and secure its placement with a dab of glue stick. Do not use pins with ultrasuede because they will leave holes.

To sew the piece in place, use a fine matching thread and sew through the raw edge with tiny stitches, just catching the cut edge. The finished piece will have a nice puffed look. The appliqué can be enhanced with an outline, stem, or chain stitch

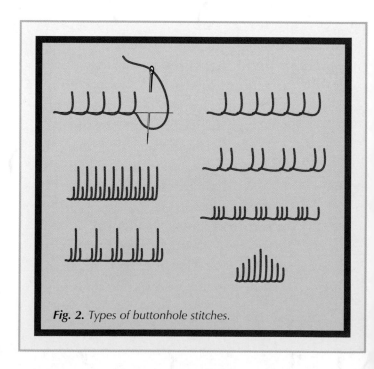

Fig. 2. *Types of buttonhole stitches.*

that follows the edge of the ultrasuede shape (Figure 3). The embroidery adds an extra touch to the piece and finishes the appliqué in an interesting manner (Figure 4).

If you prefer, the cut edge of ultrasuede can be couched (see page 20) with a decorative thread or other trim. Sew the couching or trim with matching thread. The method is quick and easy, and it allows you to use threads and trims that are too large to be threaded through the eye of a needle. Save all ultrasuede scraps. They can be used for tiny details.

Machine appliqué

Machine appliqué can be done with raw edges or with turned edges. For raw-edge appliqué, the design is cut on the pattern line with no turn-under allowance. For turned-edge appliqué, add a ⅛" to ³⁄₁₆" turn-under allowance by eye as you cut out the fabric piece.

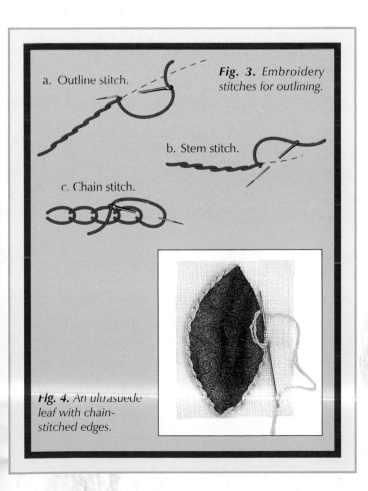

a. Outline stitch.

Fig. 3. *Embroidery stitches for outlining.*

b. Stem stitch.

c. Chain stitch.

Fig. 4. An ultrasuede leaf with chain-stitched edges.

Raw edge. With raw-edge appliqué, fraying can be prevented in several ways.

1. Apply a fusible web to the back of the fabric before cutting the piece.

2. Use a liquid fusible product on the edges after cutting the piece.

3. Use a tight buttonhole machine stitch around the edges to sew the appliqué in place.

Many people do not like to use fusible web under their fabric because it is stiff and hard to quilt. To solve this problem, you can use a narrow strip of fusible web only around the edges of the appliqué.

Turned edge. This method is similar to needle-turn, except your needle is on the sewing machine instead of in your hand. Cut the fabric shape with a scant ¼" turn-under allowance. Turn the allowance under. Secure the appliqué to the background with a hand basting stitch, basting glue, or freezer paper. Finally, secure the appliqué to the background with a machine stitch. One of the most invisible stitches you can use for securing appliqué pieces is the blind-hem stitch sewn with nylon (invisible) thread (size .004).

If you prefer, you can use a decorative machine stitch to sew the appliqué. It's best to select one of the simple stitches, such as the zigzag. Before you use a more complex stitch, consider how curvy the edges are. Will you be able to control your machine? The easier the appliqué shapes and curves, the more complex the decorative stitch can be.

Free motion. Here is another method for securing the appliqué edges whether raw or turned. Put a darning foot on your machine and drop the feed dogs, then free-motion stitch around the appliqué edge.

APPLIQUÉ SUPPLIES

Gather the following supplies to create your garden bouquets:

Freezer paper for pattern transfer.

Dress-maker's **carbon transfer paper**.

Light box (or window) for pattern transfer.

Markers: regular and colored pencils, pens, chalk, temporary and permanent fabric markers, fine-point gold and silver markers.

Fabric eraser.

Stapler.

Masking tape: ¾" and 1".

Clear plastic template material.

Rulers: straight ruler 3" x 18"; 12½" and 16½" square.

Rotary cutter and mat.

Sharp scissors to cut through 8 layers of paper and fabric.

Fine embroidery scissors.

A little garden square and wall'd;
And in it throve an ancient evergreen,
A yew-tree, and all round it ran a walk
Of shingle, and a walk divided it.

Alfred, Lord Tennyson

SNOWFLAKE MEDALLION

Stitched by Fern Junilla, Centerville, MA. In this interpretation, a frosty floral fabric was machine appliquéd to a hand-painted snowy sky. Silver metallic thread enhances the frosty look. Change the seasons by changing the fabric combinations. Pattern 10.

Threads to match appliqué fabrics, or a basic set of neutrals: fine cotton, silk-covered cotton, or pure silk thread.

A variety of **embroidery floss** colors.

Decorative threads for machine work.

Invisible nylon thread for machine appliqué.

For stems and wreaths: **trims, floss, cording**.

Needles: milliner's (straw) needles for appliqué and dimensional flowers; beading needles; an assortment of embroidery, crewel, and tapestry needles for decorative sewing.

Pins: quilt, appliqué, silk, safety.

Stabilizers: fusibles, crinoline for ribbon work. If crinoline cannot be found, try a tear-away stabilizer.

PATTERNS

As I work among my flowers, I find myself talking to them, reasoning and remonstrating with them, and adoring them as if they were human beings. Much laughter I provoke among my friends by doing so, but that is of no consequence. We are on such good terms, my flowers and I!

Celia Thaxter

REEL VARIATION I

Stitched by Elizabeth Devlin, Falmouth, MA. With the green batik appliqué mounted on point against the large-scale floral background in decorator cloth, you can almost feel the leaves brushing against the flowers. Pattern 5.

MARTHA WASHINGTON'S WREATH

Stitched by the author. A braided chenille trim serves as the wreath's stem. Teacup ribbon roses with beaded centers are nestled between marbleized blue trumpet flowers. Pattern 30.

BLOCK SIZE

The average block is 16" with a 12" appliqué. Of course, with a large-scale floral background, you could enlarge the design and have a 22" to 24" block quite easily. Be generous with your background fabrics. They can always be cut down to size after you determine what you will be doing with the completed block.

Use the patterns as given for a 12" design area, enlarge them for a four-block quilt, or reduce them for a miniature version. Reduced patterns can also be used for redwork embroidered pieces, in which case, the background fabric must be light enough to see the embroidery work. If you are making your blocks on point, allow a bit more background fabric so the pattern has ample centering space.

Marylou McDonald of Laurel, Maryland, likes to work in small scale. She reduced the patterns she liked to a 6" design area and appliquéd them on 8" background blocks (see My Garden Quilt, page 99). Her background and appliqué fabrics are coordinated for a very gentle look. The center medallion was inspired by a quilt made in New York in 1847. Marylou originally thought she would do just a four-block wallhanging, but her garden choices grew faster than her space. The solution was to reduce the pattern size to fit more blocks in the same space. These small-scale blocks stitch up in much less time than the full-sized versions.

Block patterns
Paper-cut motifs, pages 36 – 43
Garden maze, pages 44 – 48
Crossed sprays, pages 49 – 59
Wreaths, pages 60 – 76
Bouquets and blossoms, pages 77 – 97

MARKING THE BACKGROUND

Test the marking tools on your fabrics to be sure that the marks can be erased. Rather than erase appliqué turn lines, you can simply turn them under when you turn the edges. A hard-lead mechanical pencil works great for marking light-colored fabrics. Use a gold fine-point pen or chalk pencil for dark fabrics.

Trace the pattern on tracing paper or freezer paper, or photocopy it, so you will have a flat master pattern. If the pattern has more than one section, be sure to align the sections as follows: When tracing, use the marked fold lines and centering point on the pattern as placement guides. Rotate the pattern as needed to trace all the sections. Press the background fabric in quarters and align the fabric fold lines with the fold lines indicated on the pattern (Figure 5, facing page).

You may need a light box or a window to trace wreath stems and the basic design directly on the background fabric. If you cannot see through the fabric for tracing, you can make a freezer-paper template of the pattern and press it on the right side of the background block. Draw around the template. If you prefer, you can use dressmaker's tracing paper placed between the pattern and the fabric. With a tracing tool designed for use with the dressmaker's paper, trace over the pattern lines. You will need to use some pressure on the tool. A chalk line will appear on the fabric.

MARKING THE APPLIQUÉS

Freezer paper can also be used as template material for marking the appliqués. For extra strength and durability, after tracing the pattern on a sheet of freezer paper, press the tracing on a second sheet of freezer paper, shiny sides together.

Fold a 12" square of freezer paper in quarters (dull side out) with sharp, even, crease lines. Mark the top quarter section with an X. Unfold the freezer paper and trace the quarter pattern on the section marked with the X. If the pattern indicates straight and bias edges, be sure to mark these on the freezer paper also. Refold the freezer paper and staple the layers together within the pattern lines to keep them from shifting during cutting. Use very sharp scissors to cut out the template through all four layers of paper.

Some of the patterns are folded in eighths. Fold a 12" square of freezer paper in quarters. Then fold the top section toward the front and the bottom section toward the back as shown in Figure 6. Place an X on the top section. Unfold the paper and trace the one-eighth pattern on the section marked with an X, taking care to keep the block's center and the fold lines aligned with the pattern. Re-fold the paper and staple within the pattern lines to keep the layers together while cutting (Figure 7). Cut the template out carefully. There are eight layers of paper.

Remove the staples and unfold the pattern. Press it, shiny side down, on top of the appliqué fabric. Be sure to align the straight and bias folds in the pattern with the corresponding folds in the fabric. Trace around the pattern with a .01 black or brown pen.

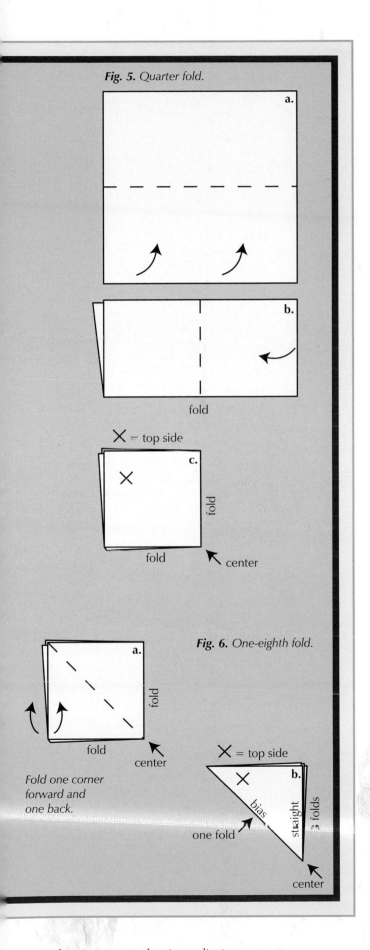

Fig. 5. *Quarter fold.*

X = top side

Fig. 6. *One-eighth fold.*

Fold one corner forward and one back.

X = top side

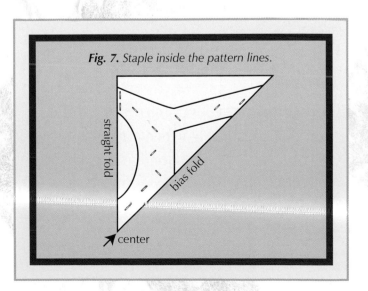

Fig. 7. *Staple inside the pattern lines.*

CUTTING THE APPLIQUÉS

Remove the freezer paper. Cut a scant ¼" (by eye) beyond the drawn line for a turn-under allowance. To make the allowance easier to turn, clip corners and curves, cutting almost to the drawn line.

If there are interior shapes to be cut out, cut a slit in the center of the shape and trim to a scant ¼" from the drawn line for a turn-under allowance (Figure 8).

Center the appliqué fabric on the background fabric, following the creased lines (Figure 9). Pin to hold in place, and baste ½" in from the drawn lines.

A template can be used whole so the appliqué shape is cut from one fabric, or the template can be cut apart into leaves and blooms, which can then be cut from different fabrics. Be sure to leave an extra ½" of fabric at the cuts for aligning the pieces.

The openings in many of the paper-cut designs lend themselves to inserting another fabric underneath them. For instance, you could use a blue fabric to represent pools of water in the garden. There is no end to the design possibilities if you cut the templates apart and cut the pattern pieces from different fabrics.

Fig. 8. Clip corners and curves.

turn–under allowance

Fig. 9. Align the appliqué folds with the background folds.

*Gardening is what we gardeners like to do:
digging, fussing with our plants,
weeding, deadheading –
all the soothing creative labors that go into
maintaining our personal Eden.*

Page Dickey

DESIGN COMPONENTS

The only limit to your garden is at the boundaries of your imagination.

Thomas D. Church

Many of the patterns in this book can be broken down into their components: stems, leaves, buds, and flowers. How you work with these components can change the original look of the pattern, but isn't this what gardening is all about?

OAK LEAVES AND BELL FLOWERS

Stitched by author. A blue autumn sky of hand-painted fabric serves as the background for this wreath of oak leaves and acorns, instead of bell flowers. The nuts are easily made from ultrasuede (page 31). Block pattern 34.

SQUARED FRAMED WREATH

Stitched by Norma MacDuff, York Beach, ME. This version represents a field of flowers. Each of the corner blooms is a printed flower cut from a large-scale chintz. The buds are chintz-printed buttons. Pattern 38.

Stems

Wreath and stem lines on the patterns are not their final width. The lines merely represent placement. It is your choice how wide a stem you would like and whether it will be stitched, embroidered, or couched. Some of the flowers in the patterns are simply drawn as circles for this same reason. You can choose a dimensional blossom, fabric-print flower, or a layered appliqué bloom. Remember, you are on a fabric adventure without any rules. Just do what seems natural and beautiful to you.

Bias strip stems

Stems can be made from bias strips cut about 1" wide. Use ¾"-wide strips for a narrower stem. Masking tape placed on the bias of a fabric makes a quick and easy cutting guide for the strips. Fold the bias strip in half along its length. Align the folded strip with the stem line in the pattern and sew the stem to the background as shown in Figure 10. Fold the strip over the stitching and blind-stitch the edge to the background to complete a stem about ¼" wide.

Fused-strip stems

Here is a quick method for making stems. Use the fused bias strips available on the market. They come in several shades of brown, green, and black, as well as other colors. They can be folded in half and ironed with the fuse side together for very narrow stems (Figure 11). These would then be couched in place.

Embroidered stems

Stems can be embroidered either by hand or machine. If by hand, a stem or outline stitch works well (see page 13), and there are many embroidery threads available. Don't hesitate to combine threads for a new look. Use one thread or more, depending on the effect you want. If you can thread it through the eye of a needle, then you should be able to embroider

with it. If you are embroidering by machine, then a narrow satin stitch would work nicely.

Couched stems

If the thread is too thick to go through a needle, then consider couching. This involves laying down a thicker thread, yarn, or cord on the drawn stem line and anchoring it in position with a thinner thread in a matching or contrasting color (Figure 12).

To work with cording, first draw a pencil line for the wreath or stem shape on the background fabric.

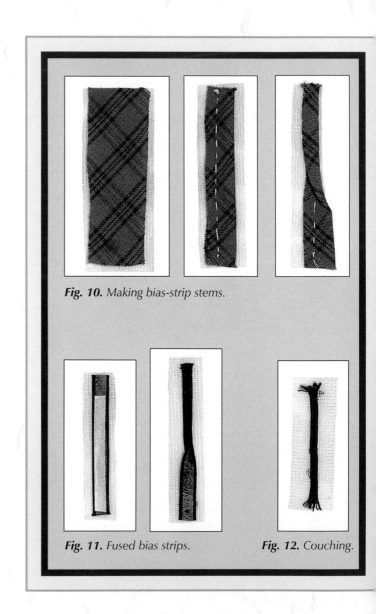

Fig. 10. *Making bias-strip stems.*

Fig. 11. *Fused bias strips.*   **Fig. 12.** *Couching.*

Then draw over this line with a thin line of white glue. A toothpick dipped in the glue provides the right amount. Then carefully place the cording over the glued line and press gently to hold. Only glue a few inches at a time because the glue does dry quickly. After it dries, you can couch the cording in place with matching or contrasting thread. Take care with selecting where the cord starts to be sure the end will be hidden under a leaf or bud.

Decorative trim stems

Decorative trims can also be used as stems and wreath circles (Figure 13). You can also use a narrow strip of ultrasuede for a stem. There is no end in sight once you start thinking of stems whenever you see anything green or brown.

LEAVES

Fabric leaves

Using a variety of greens in your leaves will add a richness to the floral blocks. Try different fabrics, such as corduroy, satin, and velvet. Use a window template to selectively cut a just-right portion of a printed fabric for a leaf. Create leaf veins with a permanent fabric pen, or embroider them with contrasting thread.

Split leaves

Consider splitting leaf patterns down the middle and using two fabrics in each leaf (Figure 14). You can use a variety of prints, solids, and textures in split leaves. When cutting a green or foliage print for a large appliqué pattern, be sure to save all the scraps. Even the smallest scrap can be used in stitching up a split leaf.

Ribbon leaves

Because of its texture and shading, French wire-edged ribbon makes wonderful leaves. Cut the leaf

pattern from the ribbon with an allowance of about 1/8". The leaf can be completely stitched down for a ribbon-work appliqué look, or you can tack it down for a raised look. Dimensional leaves are best used in wallhangings or pillows that are not used heavily.

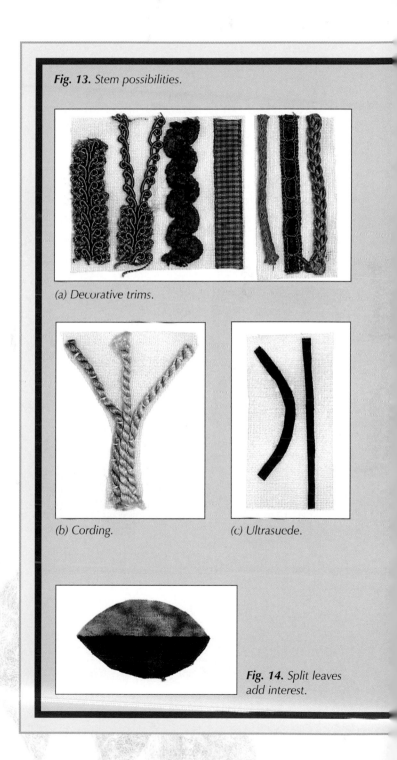

Fig. 13. Stem possibilities.

(a) Decorative trims.

(b) Cording.

(c) Ultrasuede.

Fig. 14. Split leaves add interest.

Design components

Tent leaves

Tent leaves can be made from ribbon, fabric, or decorative trims.

1. Cut the piece so its length is twice its width.

2. Fold the piece in half crosswise and pinch the wire edge to mark the center. Fold one top corner of the ribbon down to the bottom edge.

3. Fold the other top corner down to form a triangle. Using a doubled thread, sew a row of running stitches along the bottom edge, catching all layers.

4. Gather the sewn edge to create the desired leaf shape. Secure the stitches with a knot or two.

2. Fold the ribbon in half crosswise. Push on the cut edges so the wire ends poke out at the top. You may need tweezers to grab the wire.

3. Hold the wires and slide the ribbon toward the fold. Gather the ribbon on the wire as tightly as possible. Twist the wires to secure the gathers.

4. Whipstitch the two gathered edges together. Spread the halves open to form a beautiful gathered leaf.

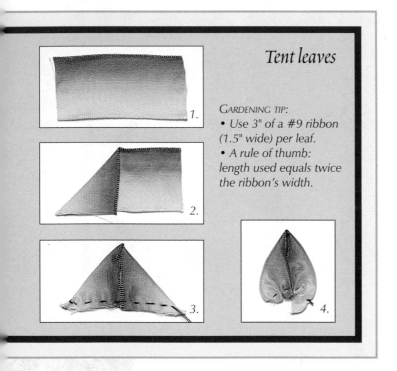

Tent leaves

GARDENING TIP:
• Use 3" of a #9 ribbon (1.5" wide) per leaf.
• A rule of thumb: length used equals twice the ribbon's width.

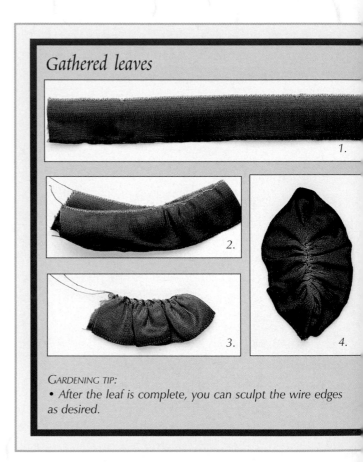

Gathered leaves

GARDENING TIP:
• After the leaf is complete, you can sculpt the wire edges as desired.

Gathered leaves

Gathered wire-edged leaves allow for sculpting along the leaf edge, for example, you can make holly leaf points along the wire edges.

1. Cut a 6" length of ¾" ribbon, size #3.

Seam-and-turn leaves

Seams can be sewn by hand, or by machine if you need to mass produce leaves for a forest quilt.

1. Choose a width for your fabric strip. One inch works nicely. The length of the piece needs to be

twice the width. When you cut the fabric strip, add ¼" to the width, which will be folded under. For our 1" example, the cut piece would be 1¼" x 2".

2. Fold the piece in half crosswise, right sides together, and sew a ¼" seam across the top.

3. Turn the piece right side out and push the center into a sharp point.

4. Using doubled thread, sew a running stitch across the bottom of the triangle.

5. Gather the leaf into the desired shape.

BUDS AND CALYXES

Simple buds

Ultrasuede calyxes and ribbon buds make a beautiful combination. The amount of ribbon or fabric used is up to you and the look you want to achieve.

1. For your first bud, try a piece of fabric or ribbon 1" by 3", size #5.

2. Using doubled thread, sew a square "U" pattern along three sides of the piece.

3. Gather the stitches tightly. The open side will become the petal color. Secure your stitches with a couple of knots.

4. Insert the bud into a calyx.

Seam-and-turn leaves

Simple buds

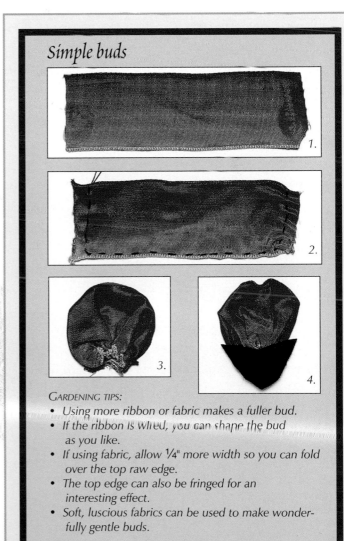

GARDENING TIPS:
- Using more ribbon or fabric makes a fuller bud.
- If the ribbon is wired, you can shape the bud as you like.
- If using fabric, allow ¼" more width so you can fold over the top raw edge.
- The top edge can also be fringed for an interesting effect.
- Soft, luscious fabrics can be used to make wonderfully gentle buds.

Design components

Calyxes

Ultrasuede. Delicate cuts from this fabric make bud calyxes easy to do.

Fabric. Cut the calyx from the pattern and use traditional appliqué to attach it to the block.

Ribbon. Fold the ribbon and wrap it around the bud. Gather the bottom edge or leave it flat.

Satin ribbon buds

For a more realistic bud, try this technique.

1. Use a 3" length of 1"-wide satin ribbon without wire.

2. Fold one side of the ribbon down. Pin to hold the fold.

3. Leaving a small opening at the point, fold the other side down and pin. Use doubled thread to sew running stitches across the bottom, through all layers.

4. Gather the ribbon tightly to form the bud.

5. Insert the bud into a calyx of ultrasuede or fabric.

Wire-edged ribbon buds

French wire-edged ribbon can also be used to make folded buds.

1. Cut a 2" length of 1"-wide wire-edged ribbon, size #5.

2. Fold the ribbon in thirds to form a triangle, leaving a small opening at the top. Use doubled thread to sew running stitches across the bottom layers.

3. Gather the ribbon tightly to form a bud.

4. To form a calyx, cut 3" of wire-edged ribbon, size #3. Fold the ribbon around a gathered or ungathered bud and secure with one stitch. Sew a running stitch across the bottom layers.

5. Gather the ribbon tightly.

Satin ribbon buds

Wire-edged ribbon buds

GARDENING TIP:
• *If a longer piece of calyx ribbon is used, a tail can be left (photos a & b).*

Fabric buds

Folded buds and calyxes can also be made from fabric.

1. Cut a 2" by 3" piece of fabric. Fold about ½" of the top edge to the wrong side and finger crease or press.

2. Fold the top corners down, leaving a small opening at the point. Sew a running stitch across the bottom through all layers.

3. Gather the strip tightly to form the bud.

4. For the calyx, cut a 2" by 3" piece of fabric. Fold the top edge as before. Use the piece to wrap the bottom of the bud and secure with a stitch.

5. Fold the bottom portion of the calyx to the back. Stitch from behind to secure the fold.

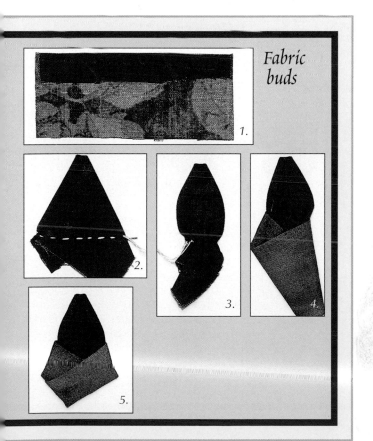

Fabric buds

1.
2.
3.
4.
5.

FLOWERS

Ruched geranium

Ruching is an old dimensional flower-making technique. It can easily be done with fabric as well as ribbon, and fabric edges can be folded over or fringed.

1. Cut an 18" length of 1½"-wide ribbon, size #9. Pin the ribbon every 1½" to make stitching guides. Use doubled thread to stitch a "W" pattern, carrying the thread over the ribbon's edges.

2. Gently gather the ribbon until you have about five petals. Arrange the petals on a small square of crinoline to form a fan shape. Sew a calyx over the bottom of the petals and stitch to secure.

Ruched geranium

1.

2.

GARDENING TIPS:
• The trick to ruching is keeping the stitched "peaks" and "valleys" equal in size. If you would like to experiment, start by sewing right angles, then experiment with narrower and wider patterns. A ¾"-wide pattern would be considered narrow; a 2" pattern, wide.
• Gather the petals every two or three peaks and valleys. If you wait too long, the thread could tangle and break.
• If you want to make a multi-layered posie, continue ruching and create a larger circle under the first one. If you run out of ribbon, just pick up another piece and continue ruching. You'll never know where it was joined once the petals have been formed.

Design components

Pointy-petal flowers

These fabric or ribbon flowers are made with units folded like the tent leaves.

1. Decide how many petals you want in your flower. For each petal, cut a piece of 1"-wide (size #5) ribbon 2" long.

2. Fold the piece in half crosswise and finger crease to mark the center. Fold the bottom corners up to form an upside-down tent shape. Using a long length of doubled thread, sew a running stitch across the top of the first petal.

3. Pick up the second petal and continue sewing. Sew all the petals together in this manner.

4. To form the gathered center, cut a 3" length of ribbon or fabric. Using doubled thread, sew a row of running stitches down the middle.

5. Gently gather the ribbon, allowing it to swirl and twirl. Leave the needle and thread attached for sewing the center to the petals.

6. Cut a circle of crinoline or stabilizer slightly larger than the flower center. Gather the petals until the circle opening is the size you want. Anchor the petals to the crinoline with a few stitches. Place the gathered center on the petals. Secure the gathers with hidden stitches.

Round petals

This versatile technique produces lovely round petals. The size of the petals will vary with the width of the ribbon or fabric strip used and the stitching distance between the petals. Don't be afraid to experiment.

1. Begin with a 6" length of ¾"-wide ribbon, size #3. Pin ½" from the cut end and at 1" intervals. End with another ½" tail.

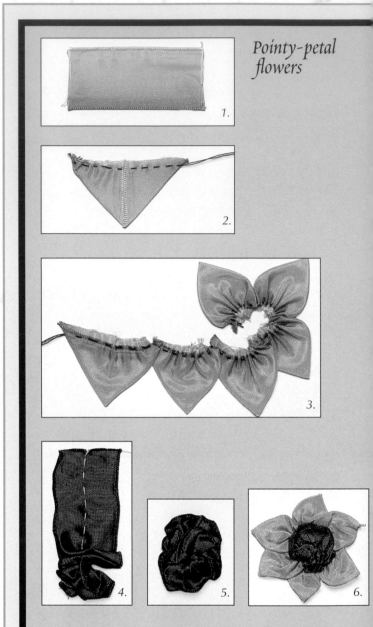

Pointy-petal flowers

GARDENING TIPS:
• Use more petals or fewer to create different flower shapes.
• Vary the size of the center opening, which does not have to be a circle. Try an oval or irregular shape for interest.
• By combining three widths of ribbon flowers into one, you can achieve a complex layered flower.
• Beads or French knots can be added to the flower center for textural variety. French knots can be made from silk buttonhole twist, embroidery floss, or 2-mm or 4-mm silk ribbon.
• Sew seed beads and larger ones in a variety of shades of gold, yellow, brown, and green in between the French knots for a sparkling effect.

2. Pencil a mark at each pin and remove the pins. Using doubled thread, begin stitching on what will become the outside edge. Remove the wire from the opposite edge. Sew down across the ribbon at the first mark, along the edge with no wire, then back up at the next mark. Be sure the thread goes over the edge at the top so the needle enters from the other side. Sew down to the bottom edge again.

3. Pull the thread to gather the petal before continuing with the next one. Do one petal at a time to avoid tangles.

4. Continue across the bottom edge, up at the next mark, over the top, then down to the bottom and pull. Continue in this manner until all the petals have been stitched. Gather each petal as tightly as possible. Sew the first petal to the last one to form a circle.

5. Mount the blossom on a small crinoline square. (A black piece was used in the sample so it would show, but white is the preferred color.) Tuck the tails into the center hole to form a padding for the beading. If the tails aren't long enough, use some scrap ribbon to fill in the empty center.

6. Fill the center with a variety of beads and French knots.

Pansy

You can use a variation on the round blossom technique to create pansies.

1. Use a 12" length of ¾"-wide French wire-edged ribbon, size #3. Cut the ribbon into a 7" and a 5" piece. Fold the 7" piece into three equal lengths and pinch the folds to mark them.

2. Unfold the ribbon and pin the crease marks. Fold the ribbon ends down at the pins. Remove the first pins and use them to repin the folds.

3. Using doubled thread, begin sewing at the inside edge of the ribbon and sew as shown.

4. Gather the ribbon tightly and secure each end with a couple of stitches.

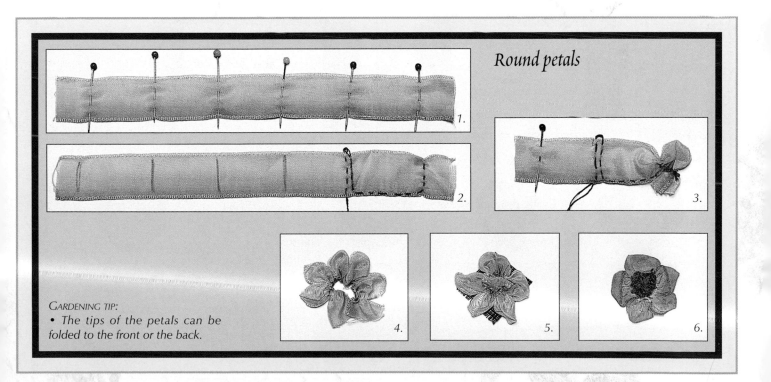

Round petals

1.

2.

3.

GARDENING TIP:
• *The tips of the petals can be folded to the front or the back.*

4.

5.

6.

Design components

5. Untwist the petals and fold them in half with the two tail ends together. Join the ends at the knots.

6. Unfold and arrange the petals to form a three-petal blossom. Be sure the top two petals lie behind the bottom petal for a realistic-looking pansy.

7. Cut a piece of narrow yellow ribbon about 4" long and tie a loose knot in it. Leave about ½" tails.

8. Insert the tails into the center opening of the pansy. Secure them with a couple of stitches.

9. Use the 5" ribbon for the back two petals. Fold the ribbon in half crosswise to find the center and mark it with a pin. Sew a square U pattern as before.

10. Pull the thread tightly to gather the two petals. There can be a little slack through the gathers for a wider petal base.

11. Arrange the two petals so they overlap slightly and sew them to one corner of a small square of crinoline.

Pansy

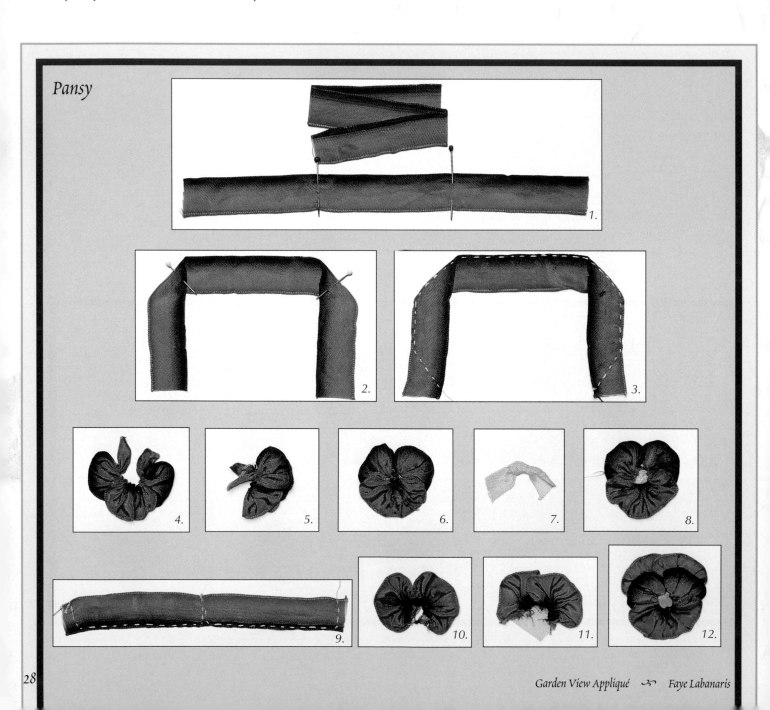

12. Place the three-petal piece on top of the two-petal piece and stitch to secure it. The result is a realistic five-petal pansy.

Teacup rose

These roses are foolproof when made with French wire-edged ribbon. You really can't go wrong with the "cup-and-saucer" construction method.

1. Use 12" of ⅝" ribbon, size 3. Expose the wire from one edge at both ends. Pull the wire out to about 2", then slightly bend it so it won't escape back into the ribbon.

2. Starting at one end and working toward the middle, gather the ribbon on the wire as tightly as possible. Then do the other side. Wrap the wire several times around the ribbon at each end to secure the gathers.

3. Fold about 1" of one end down at a right angle to the gathers and wrap the end with wire to make a stem.

4. To form the "cup," hold the stem and roll the ribbon up, keeping the gathered edge aligned. Stop when you have about 2" of gathered ribbon left, which will be used for the "saucer."

5. Gently wrap the saucer loosely around the cup, which can be as tight or as loose as you like.

6. Mount the blossom on a small square of crinoline with a few stitches. Arrange the petals with folded edges for a realistic rose effect.

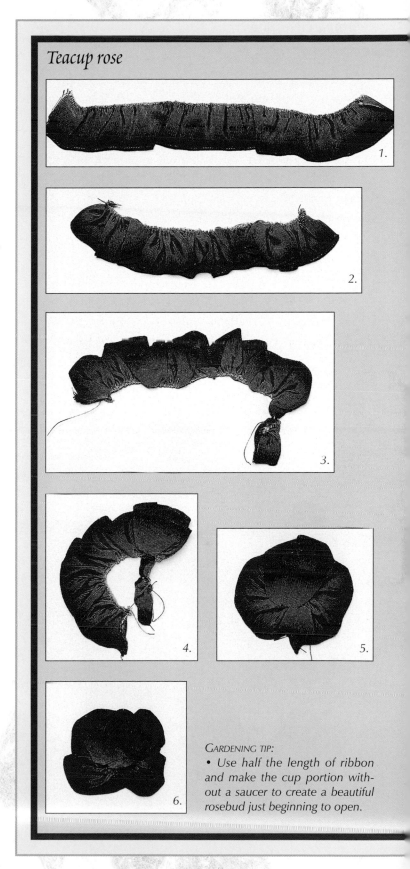

Teacup rose

GARDENING TIP:
• *Use half the length of ribbon and make the cup portion without a saucer to create a beautiful rosebud just beginning to open.*

Design components

Simple circle flowers

1. Fold an 8" length of 1"-wide (size #5) French wire-edged ribbon in half and expose the wire at each end of one side.

2. Gather the ribbon as tightly as possible. Wrap the wire around the gathers at each end. Sew the raw edges together with tiny running stitches.

3. Unfold the piece to form a flat circle. Sew the center opening to a small square of crinoline.

4. To form a swirled flower, pin the crinoline to a stable surface. (I pin it to my skirt or pants leg.) Take hold of the outer part of the petals with two hands and twirl the flower as if you were turning the steering wheel of your car. You'll soon catch on and know how much to twirl or twist.

5. Fill the center with an assortment of embroidered French knots and beads.

Berries

Consider enhancing your appliquéd block with beaded berries instead of blossoms or buds.

1. For a wonderful raspberry or blackberry, draw a ½" circle on a square of crinoline.

2. Using red or black beads (larger than seed beads), sew a circle of beads on the drawn line with matching doubled thread.

Simple circle flowers

GARDENING TIPS:
- *If you use red ribbon and a black center, the resulting flower is a poppy.*
- *To make a larger poppy, use a 12" length of ribbon, size #9.*

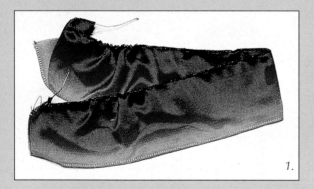
1.

2.

3.

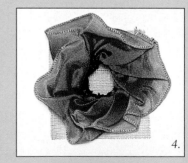
4.

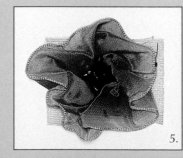
5.

3. Fill in the circle with more beads.

4. Continue adding more beads until you have stitched a heap of beads. When the berry is to your liking, add just one more for good measure.

5. Turn the berry over and trim the crinoline into a square, leaving about ½" beyond the stitched berry. Fold the crinoline toward the center and secure it with stitches. Use the crinoline square to anchor your berry to the block.

Acorns

Use two different colors of ultrasuede to make these delightful acorns.

1. Make templates from the patterns on page 67. Trace the templates on the wrong side of the ultrasuede, which is the darker side. Mark the wrong side with an X.

2. Cut out the pieces and turn them over so the X is on the back. Position the acorn pieces on the block with glue stick. Sew the acorns around the edges with matching thread.

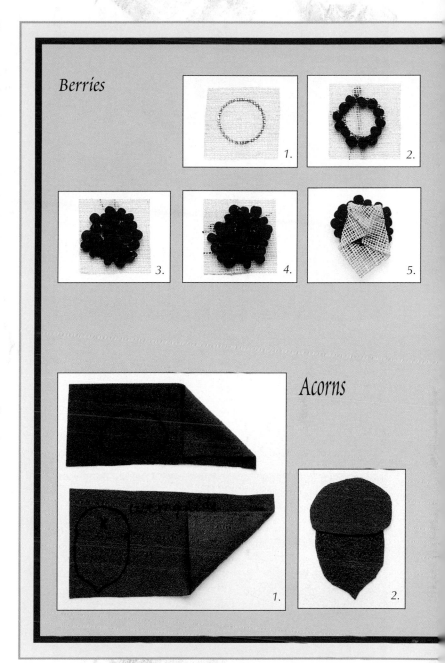

Berries

Acorns

ROSE TREE II

Stitched by Elizabeth Devlin, Falmouth, MA. You can almost feel the rose tree growing. The blossoms are circles of silk with narrow ruched edges. The gathered center is surrounded with black French knots. Pattern 42.

TULIPS II

Stitched by the author. In this block, a window template was used to select the tulips from the marbleized red fabric. You can make the leaves another color and change the center "courtyard" area, too. Pattern 7.

PLANTING YOUR GARDEN

"Sometimes since I have been in the garden I've looked up through the trees at the sky and I have had a strange feeling of being happy as if something were pushing and drawing and making me breathe fast. Magic is always pushing and drawing and making things out of nothing. Everything is made out of magic, leaves, and trees, flowers and birds, badgers and foxes, squirrels and people. So it must be all around us. In this garden — in all places."

Frances Hodgson Burnett
"The Secret Garden,"
1849 – 1924

Think of this adventure as planting a garden. The size of your garden quilt can be anywhere from one block to all the blocks in this book. You can be a successful gardener with only a flowerpot on a window ledge, as long as you love what you are doing and are happy with the end result. The following suggestions may get you started.

BLOCK GARDENS

One block
One block alone can become a complete quilt. By framing it with a variety of fabrics and widths, you can stretch this one block into a large quilt.

Two or three blocks
Sew two or three blocks in a row for a great stairwell quilt, table runner, or seasonal wall banner.

Four blocks
Combine different blocks for a theme quilt, or repeat one block four times for a traditional effect. Enlarge the blocks for maximum effect without all the stitching; for example, use a 20" to 24" background fabric instead of 16" to 18".

Nine blocks
Use nine blocks set three by three as the beginning of a medallion quilt. The center block can be the focus, framed by eight blocks.

A dozen blocks
This three-block by four-block set lends itself to a lap- or bed-sized quilt. Simply add enough borders to create the size you want.

The full bouquet
Keep making as many blocks as you like and alternate them with floral or green block-sized squares to complete the full bouquet. Add a wide border cut from a lush floral fabric to create a large quilt in no time.

FENCING AND PATHWAYS

Sashing
Blocks can be set with sashing strips. The strips, cut in a variety of widths, can be green to resemble grass edges or other colors and prints to represent brick or stone pathways through the garden.

Framing
Once all the blocks have been sewn together, they can be framed with a 2" to 3"-wide strip to resemble a hedgerow or a floral border, or you can use a brick or stone fabric to create the appearance of a wall. Brick fabric can also be cut and stitched into a dogtooth border to represent a brick edging. You can go one step further with this and fold fabric squares into prairie points for a dimensional brick edge.

The border strip can be a very wide piece of a large scale floral fabric for a wholecloth border. Many wonderful decorator and chintz fabrics are perfect for this type of border treatment. You can also use green to represent a large lawn area surrounding your floral garden or green hedges. Bali batiks are wonderful in this manner. The border can also have appliquéd vines and leaves meandering around it. Think of the fun you can have with all these borders. You can make a small one- to four-block set grow into a bed-sized quilt simply by adding more fabric.

> *I think there are as many kinds of gardens as of poetry.*
>
> John Addison
> English poet, 1672–1719

BACKYARD ART

Don't forget the back of the quilt. A single floral or green fabric could be used. The green would definitely show off all your quilting designs. It's okay if the threads used on the front are different colors. That would make the green back more exciting. You could also try a backing made of floral squares, perhaps pieced in a large-scale pattern resembling a watercolor quilt. Create a garden that goes all the way around the quilt, front to back.

This kiss of the sun for pardon,
the song of the birds for mirth,
one is nearer God's heart in a garden
than anywhere else on earth.

Dorothy Frances Gurney

SQUARE WREATH OF ROSES

Stitched by Linda Tonyes, Marlton, NJ. This elegant wreath is a joy to stitch. The roses are made from wire-edged ribbon, flattened to resemble pressed Victorian roses. Pattern 35.

GARDEN ORNAMENTS

Beautify your garden with quilting designs inspired by the fabrics you used or by nature. Make simple sketches or tracings of foliage, flowers, and vines. Add straight-line quilting to resemble the sun's rays.

Enhance the fabric designs with beadwork. Add embroidery stitches with decorative threads or silk ribbon to outline flowers in the fabrics.

Even the label can be a miniature garden with ink work, beading, embroidery, and floral fabrics. You can begin your label even before you've finished the quilt.

Being happy is dirt under your fingernails,
wearing old clothes, having a good idea get
better the longer you work at it,
starting a new bed, giving plants away,
and listening to rain.

Geoffrey B. Charlesworth

BLOCK PATTERNS

ROSE I
Stitched by Barbara Flkhorn, York, ME. A soft gray-green background provides strong contrast for the flower. A variety of green leaves adds interest to this dramatic block. Pattern 43.

The patterns presented here were selected from vintage quilt and block collections from the 1800s and early 1900s. Patterns were collected and passed down within families and among friends. Sometimes, the original name stayed with the pattern, and other times, the name was changed as the pattern changed with variations of the design elements. Appliqué patterns varied in their construction, depending on the skill and whim of the maker. I have included, when available, the original name of the pattern. If I could not find a name, then I christened the block with a new one and included it in quotation marks. After all, a rose by any other name would smell as sweet.

"BLOOMING HEARTS I"
Stitched by Rosemary Maciolek, Lee, NH. The sharp contrast of a light floral on a dark green background defines the beauty of this pattern. Pattern 9.

PAPER-CUT PATTERNS

*The love of gardening is a seed
that once sown never dies.*

Gertrude Jekyll

Paper-cut designs in the early album quilts are very common and are attributed to the German immigrants who settled in Pennsylvania in the 18th and 19th centuries. The Pennsylvania Deutch, or Dutch as they were called, were skilled in paper-cutting designs both simple and complex. These are fun to create. Try your hand at varying some of these paper-cut patterns. If you don't like the design, just toss it away. All you have to lose is paper.

REEL VARIATION II
Stitched by Brenda Pergerson, Barrington, NH. This block takes on a new look with the addition of a marbleized blue fabric for a pool center. Go one step further by replacing the center green diamond area with a fabric of stones or bricks. Pattern 5.

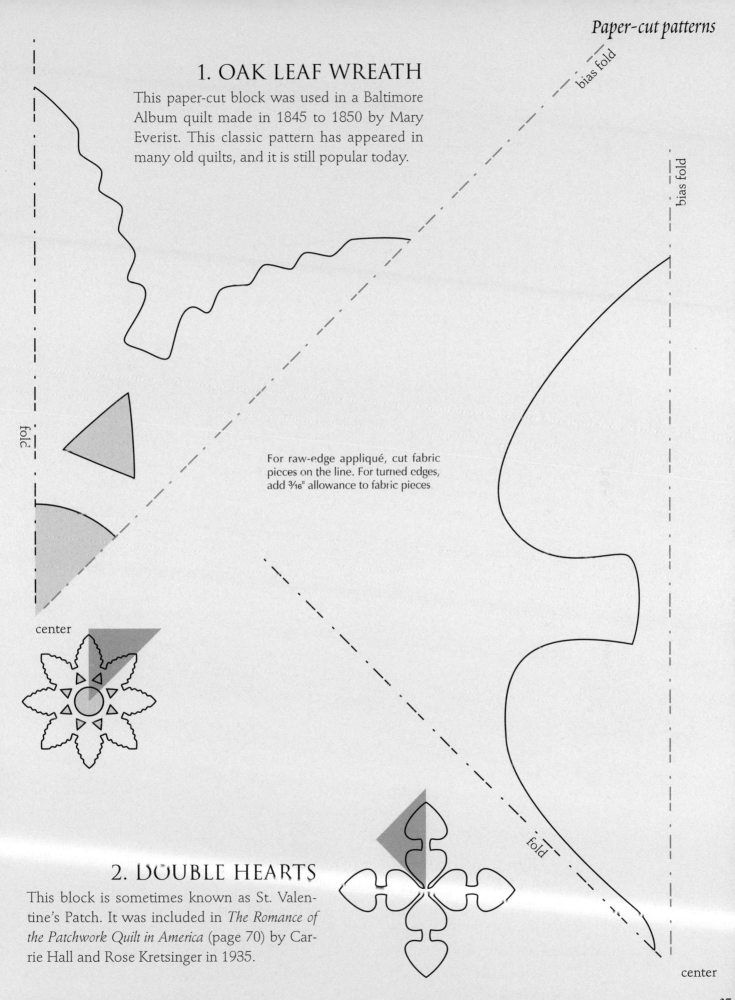

1. OAK LEAF WREATH

This paper-cut block was used in a Baltimore Album quilt made in 1845 to 1850 by Mary Everist. This classic pattern has appeared in many old quilts, and it is still popular today.

For raw-edge appliqué, cut fabric pieces on the line. For turned edges, add 3/16" allowance to fabric pieces

2. DOUBLE HEARTS

This block is sometimes known as St. Valentine's Patch. It was included in *The Romance of the Patchwork Quilt in America* (page 70) by Carrie Hall and Rose Kretsinger in 1935.

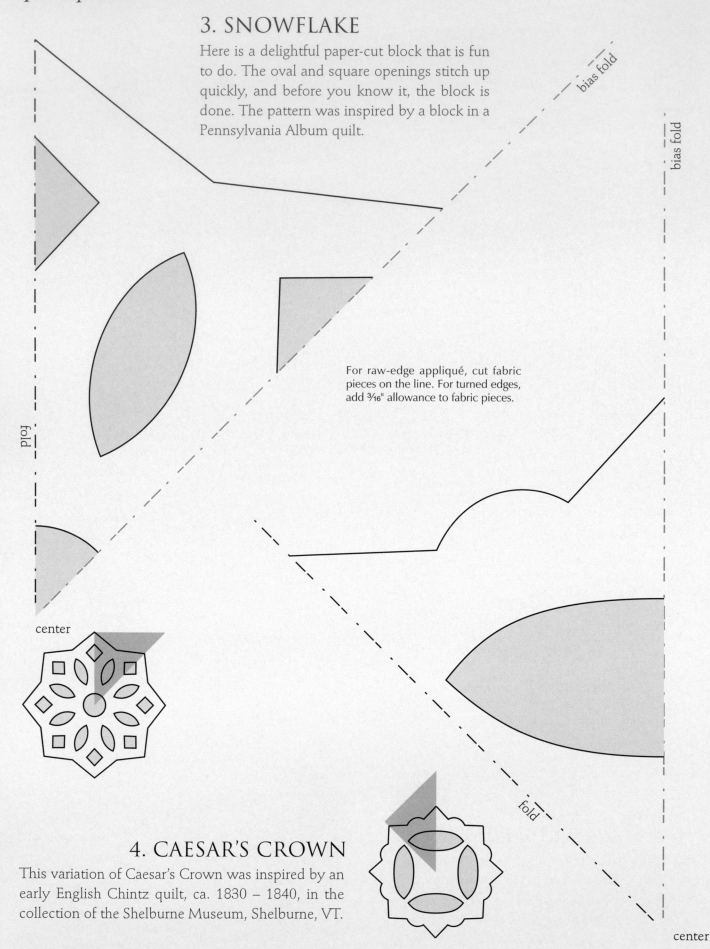

3. SNOWFLAKE

Here is a delightful paper-cut block that is fun to do. The oval and square openings stitch up quickly, and before you know it, the block is done. The pattern was inspired by a block in a Pennsylvania Album quilt.

For raw-edge appliqué, cut fabric pieces on the line. For turned edges, add ³⁄₁₆" allowance to fabric pieces.

center

fold

bias fold

bias fold

fold

4. CAESAR'S CROWN

This variation of Caesar's Crown was inspired by an early English Chintz quilt, ca. 1830 – 1840, in the collection of the Shelburne Museum, Shelburne, VT.

center

5. REEL VARIATION

This popular pattern is only slightly more complex than Turkey Tracks. A few extra snips of paper and a new pattern develops.

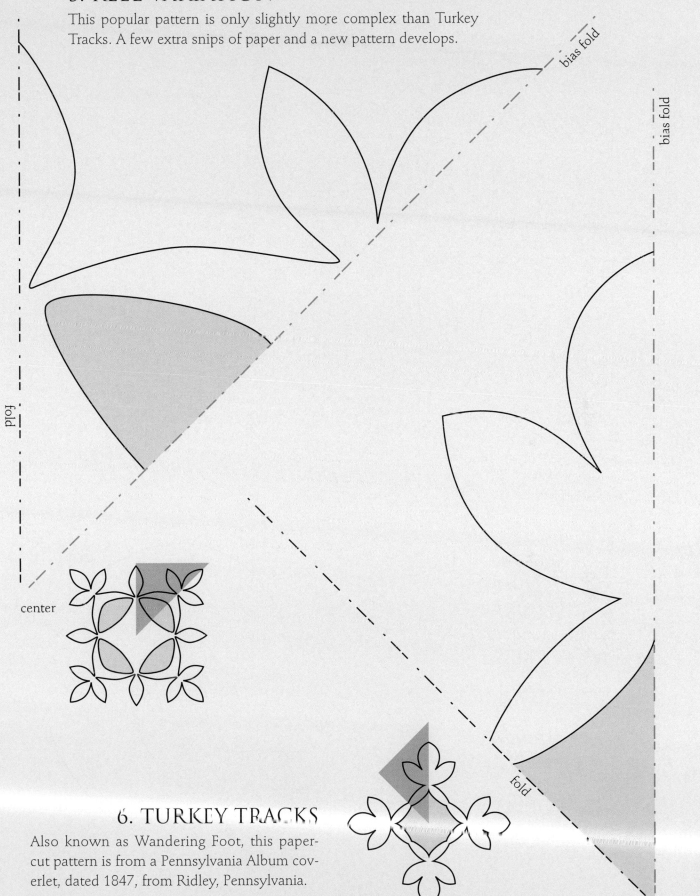

bias fold

bias fold

fold

center

fold

center

6. TURKEY TRACKS

Also known as Wandering Foot, this paper-cut pattern is from a Pennsylvania Album coverlet, dated 1847, from Ridley, Pennsylvania.

7. TULIPS

The inspiration for Tulips was a Baltimore Album quilt, circa 1850, whose maker is unknown. The original was most likely a Pennsylvania Dutch paper-cut pattern.

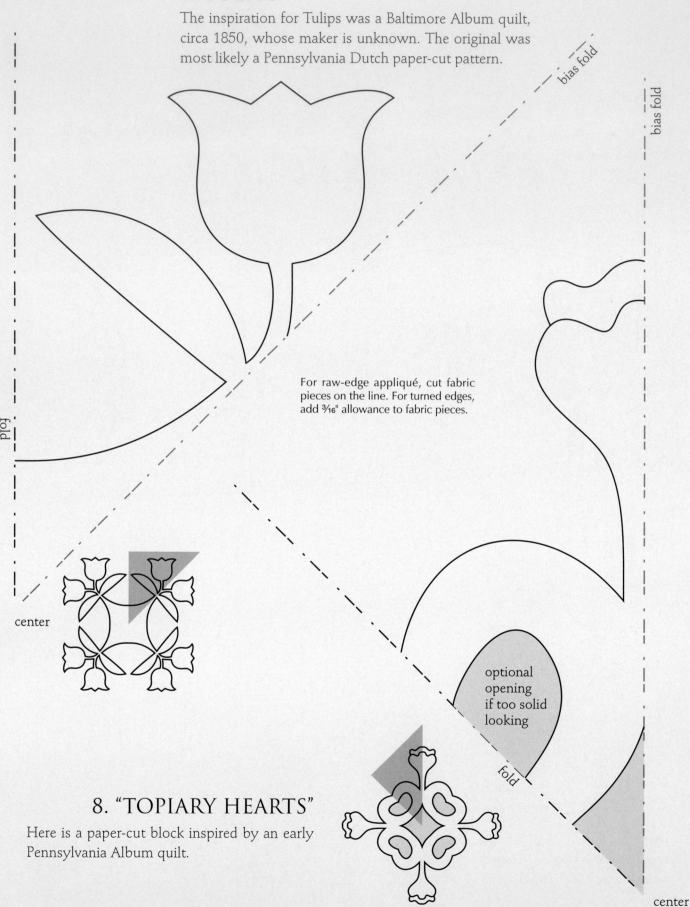

bias fold

bias fold

For raw-edge appliqué, cut fabric pieces on the line. For turned edges, add ³⁄₁₆" allowance to fabric pieces.

fold

center

optional opening if too solid looking

fold

8. "TOPIARY HEARTS"

Here is a paper-cut block inspired by an early Pennsylvania Album quilt.

center

9. "BLOOMING HEARTS"

A paper-cut block like this can be seen on an early Maryland unfinished quilt top that was made about 1850.

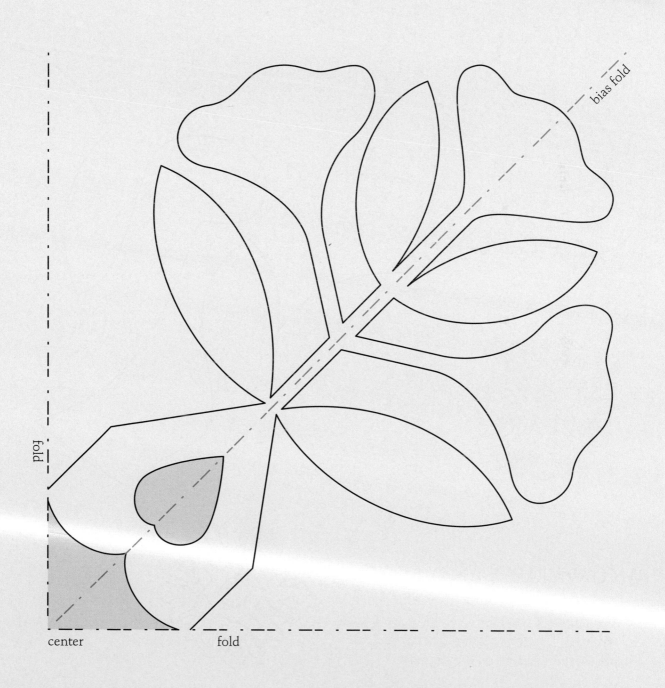

bias fold

fold

center   fold

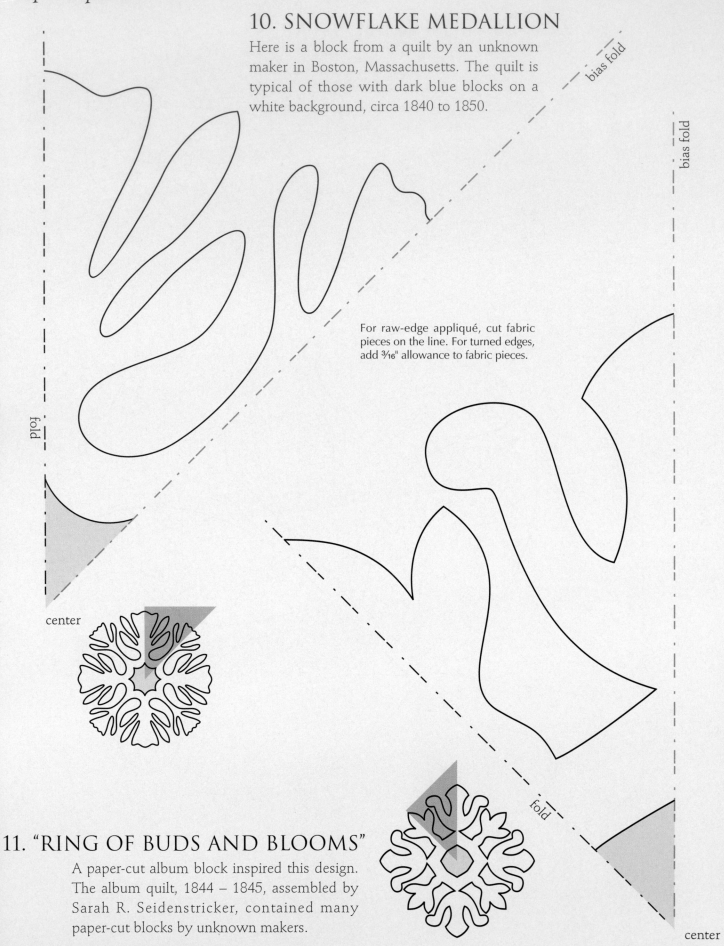

10. SNOWFLAKE MEDALLION

Here is a block from a quilt by an unknown maker in Boston, Massachusetts. The quilt is typical of those with dark blue blocks on a white background, circa 1840 to 1850.

bias fold

bias fold

fold

For raw-edge appliqué, cut fabric pieces on the line. For turned edges, add ³⁄₁₆" allowance to fabric pieces.

center

fold

11. "RING OF BUDS AND BLOOMS"

A paper-cut album block inspired this design. The album quilt, 1844 – 1845, assembled by Sarah R. Seidenstricker, contained many paper-cut blocks by unknown makers.

center

12. GARDEN FLEURS

This fleur-de-lis variation came from a paper-cut Album quilt made by a member of the Darlington family, circa 1866, in the Doylestown, Pennsylvania area.

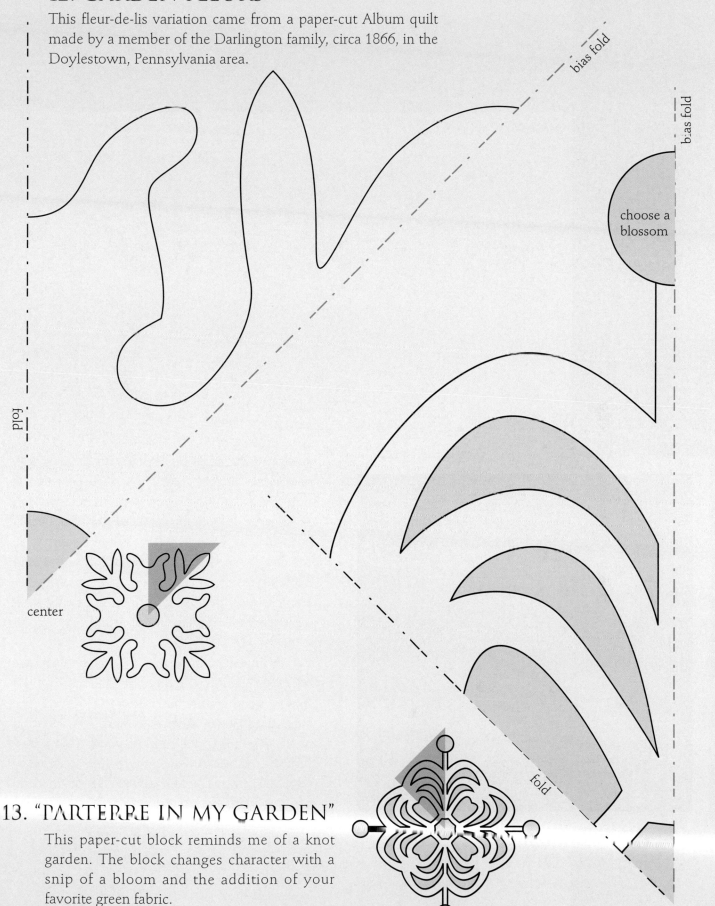

bias fold

bias fold

choose a blossom

fold

center

bias fold

fold

center

13. "PARTERRE IN MY GARDEN"

This paper-cut block reminds me of a knot garden. The block changes character with a snip of a bloom and the addition of your favorite green fabric.

GARDEN MAZE SERIES

These four patterns are designs for architectural, geometric, or fancy gardens so popular in the nineteenth century. They were inspired by an 1842 gardening book, *Encyclopedia of Cottage, Farm and Villa*, by John Oberlin. When I saw these designs, I thought of how beautiful they would be paper-cut to represent knot gardens. With different fabrics, they can also look like trellis work against a floral or foliage background.

For technical help on this type of pattern, see page 16, Marking the appliqués. If you would like to needle-turn the following designs, be sure to add turn-under allowances. A variation of these patterns will result if you cut your pattern and fabric on the drawn line instead of adding a turn-under allowance. Use this method only if you are an experienced appliquér because it will present a challenge to you.

"FLEUR-DE-LIS WITH HEARTS AND DIAMONDS"

Classic patterns of garden design transfer into dynamic paper-cut designs when stitched in beautiful fabrics.

14. "STAR OF HEARTS"

The simple format of a circle in a square is accented with a ring of hearts surrounding a center star.

For raw-edge appliqué, cut fabric pieces on the line. For turned edges, add ³⁄₁₆" allowance to fabric pieces.

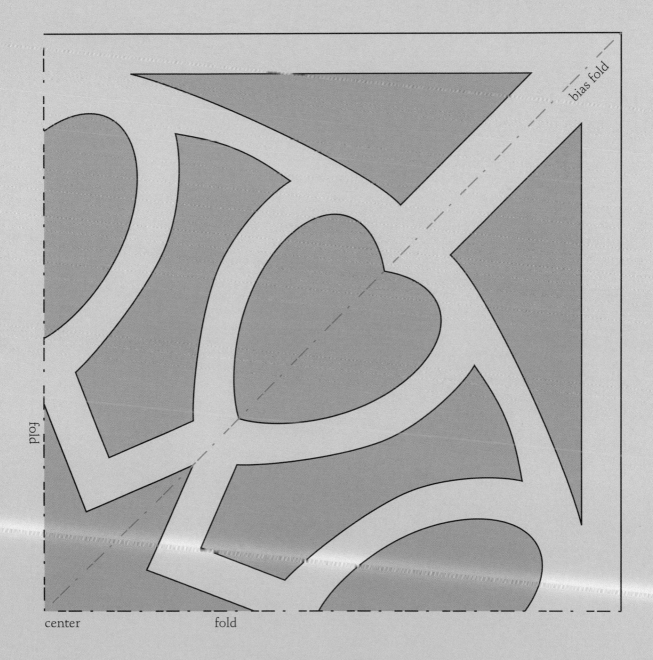

15. "SHAMROCK CORNERSTONES"

This basic square-within-a-square format is accented with four cornerstone shamrocks as well as a centerpiece shamrock. A leaf design radiating from the center completes the design.

For raw-edge appliqué, cut fabric pieces on the line. For turned edges, add ³⁄₁₆" allowance to fabric pieces.

bias fold

fold

center   fold

16. "FLEUR-DE-LIS WITH GREEK CROSS"

Concentric circles radiate from a center circle. The corners are accented with a classic fleur-de-lis pattern.

bias fold

fold

fold

center

17. "FLEUR-DE-LIS WITH HEARTS AND DIAMONDS"

This complex pattern of radiating stars is accented with another version of the fleur-de-lis design in the corners.

For raw-edge appliqué, cut fabric pieces on the line. For turned edges, add ³⁄₁₆" allowance to fabric pieces.

bias fold

fold

center   fold

. . .God gave us memory so that we might
have roses in December.

Sir J.M. Barrie, Scottish playwright,
creator of Peter Pan, 1860 – 1937

Now we will start to bloom with this delightful series of traditional album crossed floral spray patterns. Have fun with floral fabrics as the inspirational starting points for your garden adventure.

CROSSED BERRY SPRAY

Stitched by Jeanne Zaleski, North Oxford, MA; berries by the author. Luscious blackberries and raspberries are made by dimensional beading (page 30). You can almost pick them and pop them in your mouth! Pattern 20.

18. MEADOW DAISY

This block is also called Black-Eyed Susan, another favorite wildflower. The pattern is simple to appliqué. Cut the petals from ultra-suede for a very easy appliqué.

For raw-edge appliqué, cut fabric pieces on the line. For turned edges, add ³⁄₁₆" allowance to fabric pieces.

center

19. CROSSED LAUREL SPRAY

Crossed Laurel Spray is a popular classic that has appeared in many Album quilts, both early and Baltimore style.

center

20. CROSSED BERRY SPRAY

The pattern was inspired by a Maryland Album quilt, dated 1844, possibly made by Sarah A. White.

For raw-edge appliqué, cut fabric pieces on the line. For turned edges, add ³⁄₁₆" allowance to fabric pieces.

center

21. ROSEBUD CROSS SPRAY

A Maryland Album quilt, made for Joseph Levins Mills, was the source for this charming pattern. It is a dainty beauty that can be varied by shortening the stems between the pairs of leaves to make a tighter spray of rosebuds.

center

22. WILDFLOWER SPRAY

An appliquéd Album bridal quilt made in 1851 by Elizabeth Jane Baile, Carroll County, Maryland, inspired this lovely block.

For raw-edge appliqué, cut fabric pieces on the line. For turned edges, add ³⁄₁₆" allowance to fabric pieces.

center

23. ROSE OF LE MOYNE

This is a double twisted version of a traditional pattern by Nancy Cabot, presented in the *Chicago Tribune* in 1933.

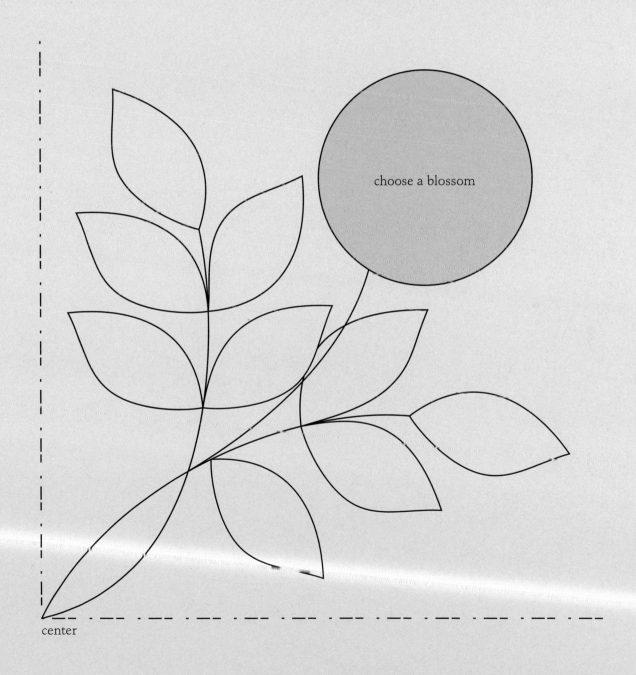

choose a blossom

center

24. SWIRLING POSIES

The Swirling Posies pattern came from a Maryland quilt that was made in 1859. The maker is unknown.

For raw-edge appliqué, cut fabric pieces on the line. For turned edges, add ³⁄₁₆" allowance to fabric pieces.

center

25. CALENDULA

The design for Calendula was sparked by an early quilt in the collection of Rose Kretsinger.

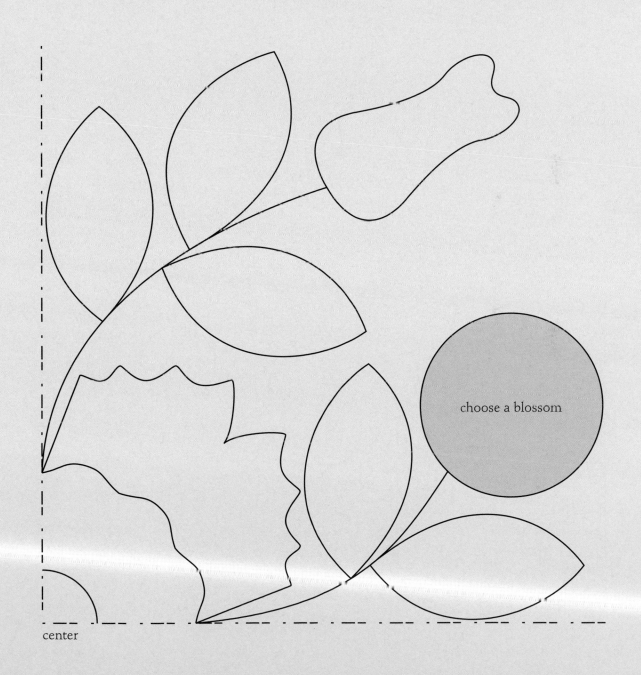

choose a blossom

center

26. OREGON ROSE

The design for this block came from an 1851 appliqué quilt made by friends, neighbors, and relatives of the Robbins family as they prepared to leave for Oregon. The original red and green appliqué is typical of Oregon Trail quilts.

For raw-edge appliqué, cut fabric pieces on the line. For turned edges, add ³⁄₁₆" allowance to fabric pieces.

center

27. OLD ENGLISH ROSE

This old pattern is a variation of Calendula (page 57) and the popular Oregon Rose. A slight change of blossoms and their placement result in a new pattern.

center

WREATHS

*If I had but two loaves of bread,
I would sell one and buy hyacinths,
For they would feed my soul.*

The Koran

From the laurel wreath worn by the first Olympians and by Caesar to the those laid at the graves of fallen heroes, the wreath has long been a symbol of respect and honor. It was only natural for quiltmakers to interpret this symbol in fabric.

From a design standpoint, the wreath has been used to break up the rigid format of the square. With the wreath structure, the quiltmaker is free to use the design elements of her choice. The wreath's simple format changes with each needleworker. Many combinations of flowers, buds, leaves, and fruit are used to create beautiful and varied wreath designs. In addition, the design of the wreath block allows large areas of background to show, providing an area to showcase fancy quilt patterns.

TULIP WREATH

Stitched by author. A springtime floral fabric serves as the background with the center removed and blue sky added. A braided green trim joins the two fabrics. Pattern 32.

28. HYACINTHS

This simple wreath design is based on a circle of paper-cut leaves, all touching each other. The result is easy to construct, and the maker has her choice of blossoms to complete this simple, yet lovely, wreath.

For raw-edge appliqué, cut fabric pieces on the line. For turned edges, add ³⁄₁₆" allowance to fabric pieces.

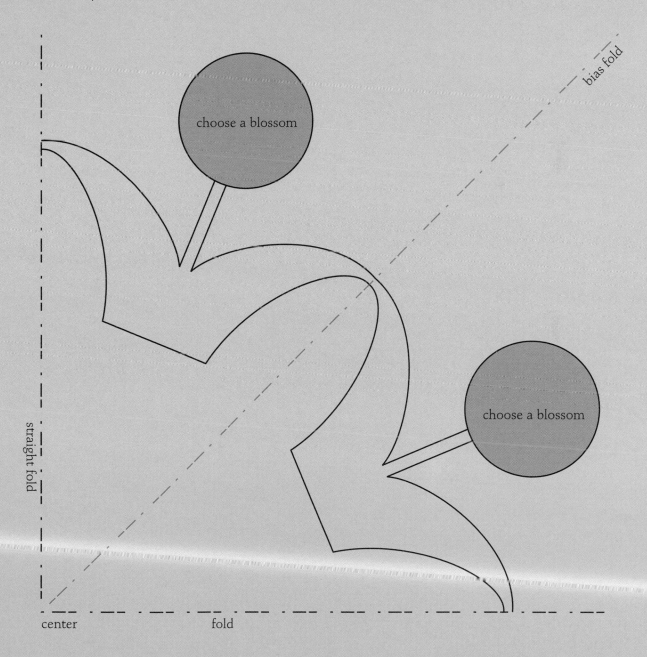

29. WREATH OF BUDS

The inspiration for this lovely wreath came from a block in a Baltimore Album quilt, circa 1847 – 1850, made by Mary Everist of Maryland.

For raw-edge appliqué, cut fabric pieces on the line. For turned edges, add 3/16" allowance to fabric pieces.

center

30. MARTHA WASHINGTON'S WREATH

As wreaths have long been a symbol of honor, the designer of this block chose to honor America's first First Lady, Martha Washington.

center

31. BLUE WREATH

This design was inspired by an 1865 quilt made by Alice Tandy of Illinois. In Alice's quilt, the smaller petals are white against the larger petals in dark blue, the color of her lover's military uniform.

For raw-edge appliqué, cut fabric pieces on the line. For turned edges, add ³⁄₁₆" allowance to fabric pieces.

center

32. TULIP WREATH

Tulip Wreath was inspired by a Baltimore Album quilt, made around 1848, whose maker is unknown.

center

33. "BERRY WREATH"

The original block appeared on a pieced and appliquéd Album quilt, dated 1844 and sewn by Sarah A. White of Maryland.

For raw-edge appliqué, cut fabric pieces on the line. For turned edges, add ³⁄₁₆" allowance to fabric pieces.

center

34. OAK LEAVES AND BELL FLOWERS

An Album bridal quilt, dated 1851, contained this intriguing block. The quilt was made by Elizabeth Jane Baile of Carroll County, Maryland. Pattern continues on next page.

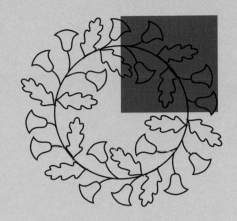

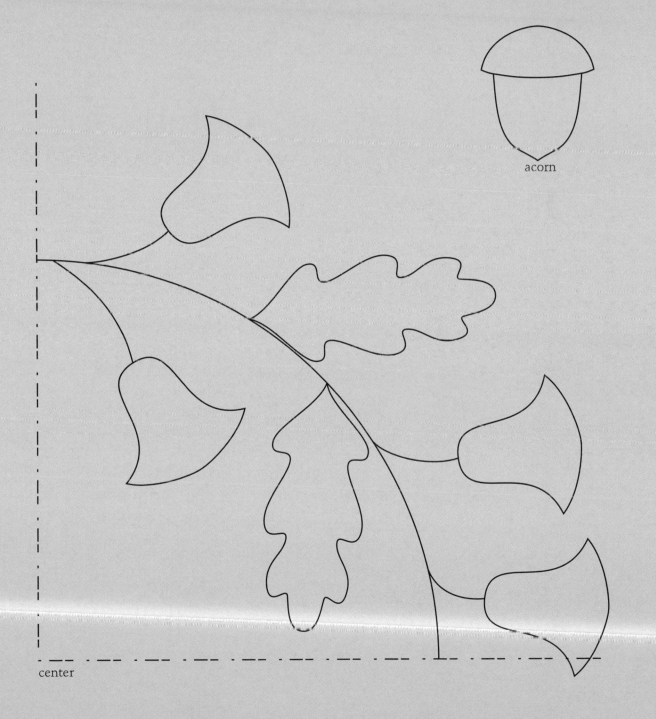

acorn

center

34. OAK LEAVES AND BELL FLOWERS continued

For raw-edge appliqué, cut fabric pieces on the line. For turned edges, add ³⁄₁₆" allowance to fabric pieces.

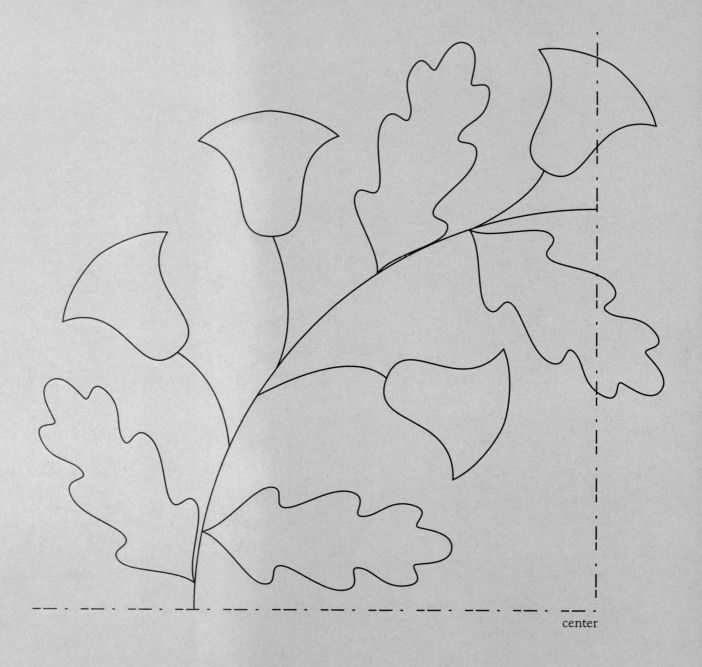

center

35. SQUARE WREATH OF ROSES

This design was inspired by the Single Rose Quilt, circa 1860, made by Julia Hayden Marshall of Greer, Ohio.

choose a blossom

center

36. ROSE WREATH

Rose Wreath came from a block in a Baltimore Album quilt, circa 1848, whose maker is unknown. Trace the two quarters of the pattern, then turn the pattern over to trace the left half.

For raw-edge appliqué, cut fabric pieces on the line. For turned edges, add 3⁄16" allowance to fabric pieces.

center

36. ROSE WREATH continued

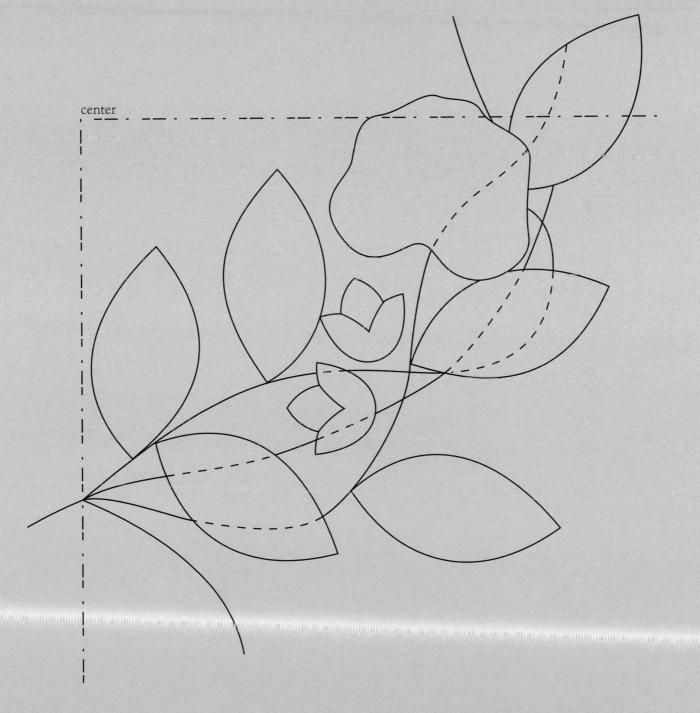

center

37. WREATH BOUQUET

The inspiration for this block was found in an 1850s Baltimore Album quilt. The maker is not known. Pattern presented in four sections, pages 72 – 75.

For raw-edge appliqué, cut fabric pieces on the line. For turned edges, add ³⁄₁₆" allowance to fabric pieces.

center

Garden View Appliqué ❧ *Faye Labanaris*

37. WREATH BOUQUET continued

center

37. WREATH BOUQUET continued

For raw-edge appliqué, cut fabric pieces on the line. For turned edges, add ³⁄₁₆" allowance to fabric pieces.

center

37. WREATH BOUQUET continued

center

38. "SQUARED FRAMED WREATH"

The quilt that inspired this block is an 1849 Baltimore Album. The maker is unknown, but it is thought that it was made for Thomas Lewis Darnell when he married Adeline Virginia Bartnoff.

For raw-edge appliqué, cut fabric pieces on the line. For turned edges, add ³⁄₁₆" allowance to fabric pieces.

Half the interest of a garden is in the Constant exercise of the imagination.

Mrs. C. W. Earle

A garden full of flowers entices one to pick a bouquet or just a single bloom to enjoy indoors or to give as a gift. And so it is with this series of patterns. Enjoy your garden created with fabrics.

ROSE II
Stitched by Rosemary Maciolek, Lee, NH. The fused rose and leaves are outlined in a buttonhole stitch on a spray-of-roses background fabric. Pattern 43.

39. MRS. KRETSINGER'S ROSE

This classic block is also known as the original Whig Rose. It would make a lovely one-block quilt.

For raw-edge appliqué, cut fabric pieces on the line. For turned edges, add ³⁄₁₆" allowance to fabric pieces.

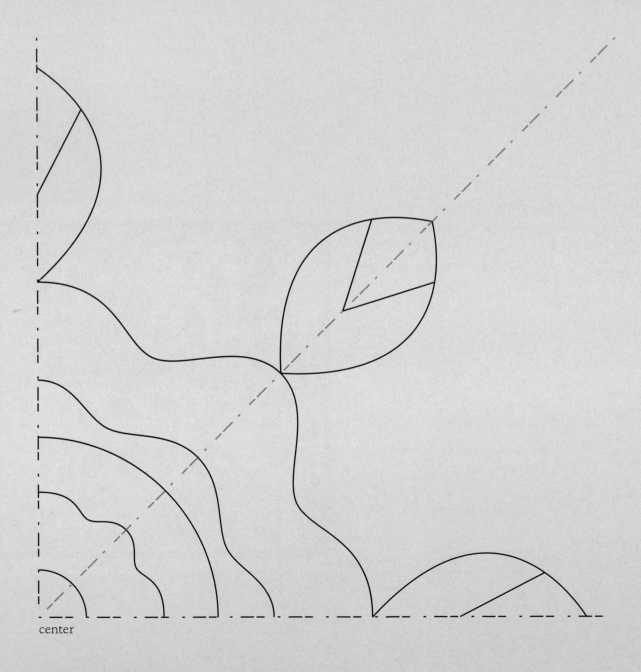

center

40. WHIG ROSE

The Whig Party was popular in the United States in the mid 1800s. Its ideals and beliefs have been honored by an early quiltmaker with this single rose design. This pattern is presented in four sections, pages 79 – 82.

center

40. WHIG ROSE continued

For raw-edge appliqué, cut fabric pieces on the line. For turned edges, add ³⁄₁₆" allowance to fabric pieces.

center

40. WHIG ROSE continued

center

40. WHIG ROSE continued

For raw-edge appliqué, cut fabric pieces on the line. For turned edges, add ³⁄₁₆" allowance to fabric pieces.

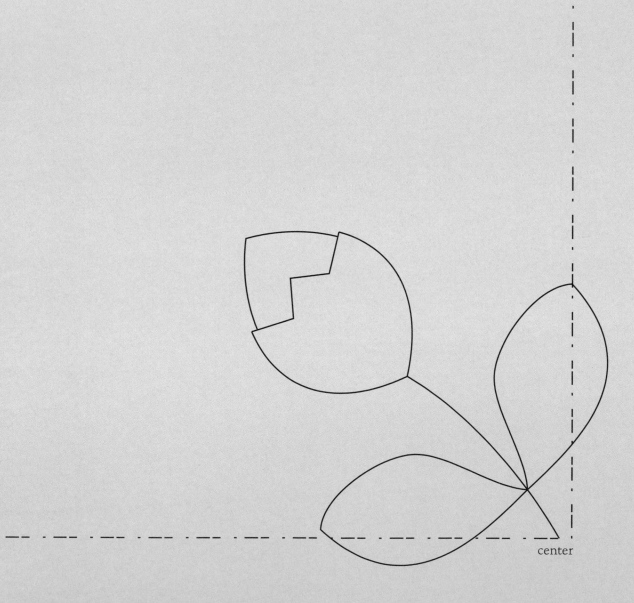

center

41. "COURTYARD URNS"

Courtyard Urns came from a block in a Baltimore Album Quilt, circa 1850, made by the Ladies of the Caroline Street Methodist Church.

center

42. ROSE TREE

This charming block was adapted from a rare old Swiss quilt. This pattern is presented in four sections, pages 84 – 87.

For raw-edge appliqué, cut fabric pieces on the line. For turned edges, add 3⁄16" allowance to fabric pieces.

center

42. ROSE TREE continued

center

42. ROSE TREE continued

For raw-edge appliqué, cut fabric pieces on the line. For turned edges, add ³⁄₁₆" allowance to fabric pieces.

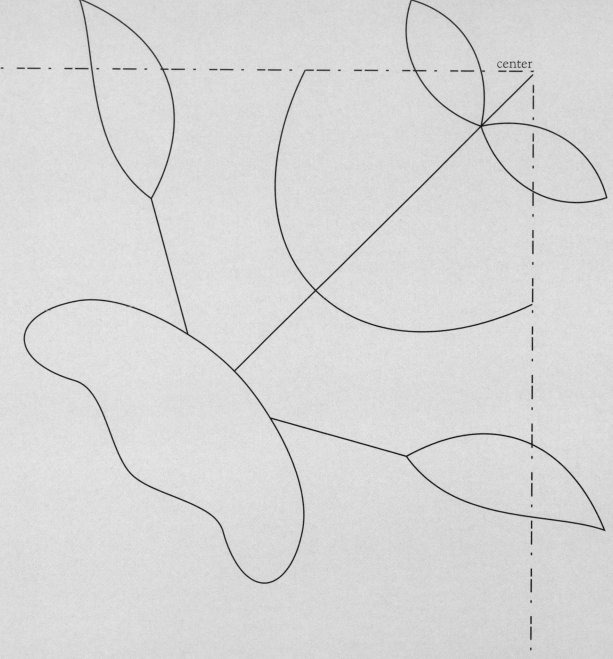

center

42. ROSE TREE continued

center

43. ROSE

This pattern was inspired by an 1860s Album quilt, whose maker is unknown. It is a contemporary interpretation of a single rose. What is a garden without roses. Even a gift of a single rose says "I love you!" This pattern is presented in four sections, pages 88 – 91.

For raw-edge appliqué, cut fabric pieces on the line. For turned edges, add ³⁄₁₆" allowance to fabric pieces.

center

43. ROSE continued

center

43. ROSE continued

For raw-edge appliqué, cut fabric pieces on the line. For turned edges, add ³⁄₁₆" allowance to fabric pieces.

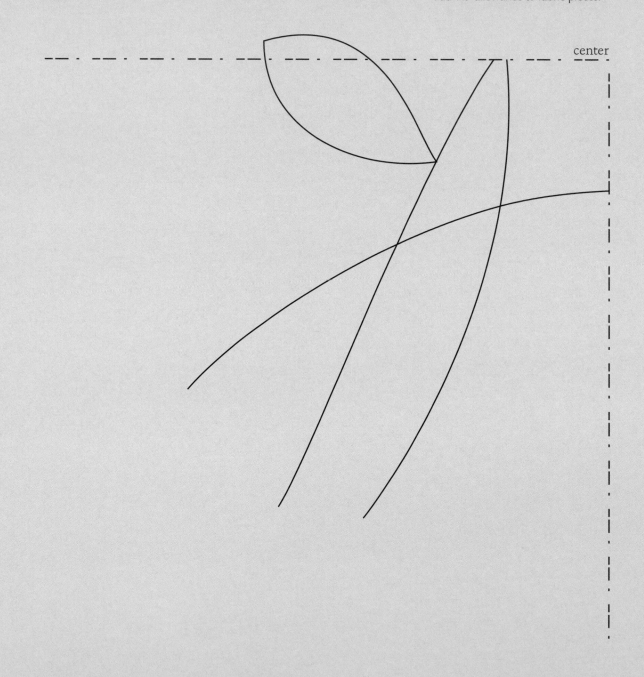

center

43. ROSE continued

center

44. "ROSE BOUQUET"

The prototype was found in a Baltimore Album Quilt, circa 1840. It was inscribed "Ellenor & Elizabeth A. Gorsuch." This pattern is presented in four sections, pages 92 – 95.

For raw-edge appliqué, cut fabric pieces on the line. For turned edges, add ³⁄₁₆" allowance to fabric pieces.

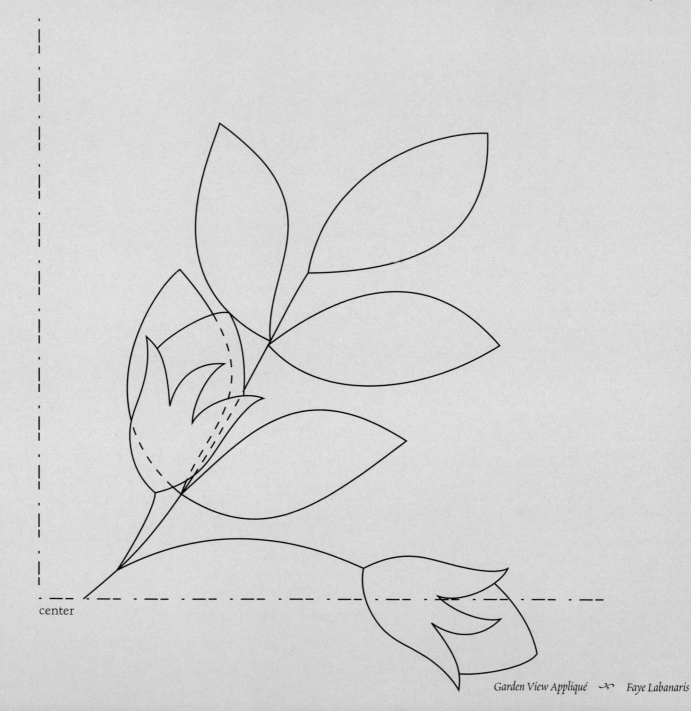

center

44. "ROSE BOUQUET" continued

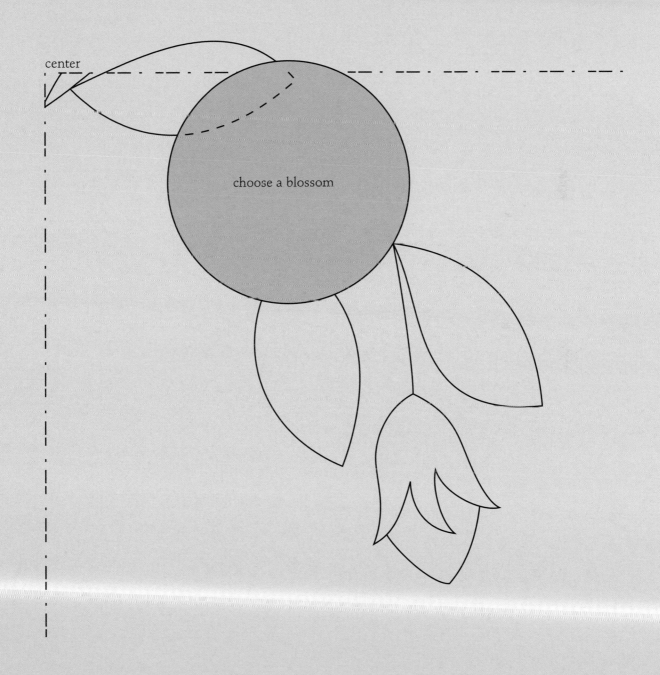

center

choose a blossom

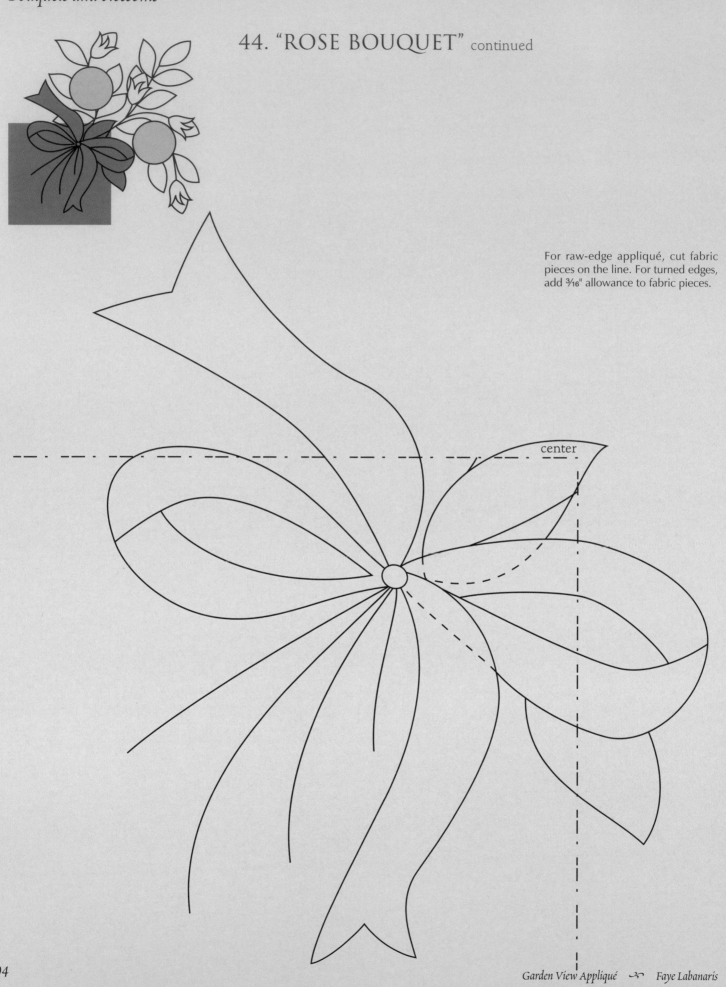

44. "ROSE BOUQUET" continued

For raw-edge appliqué, cut fabric pieces on the line. For turned edges, add 3/16" allowance to fabric pieces.

center

44. "ROSE BOUQUET" continued

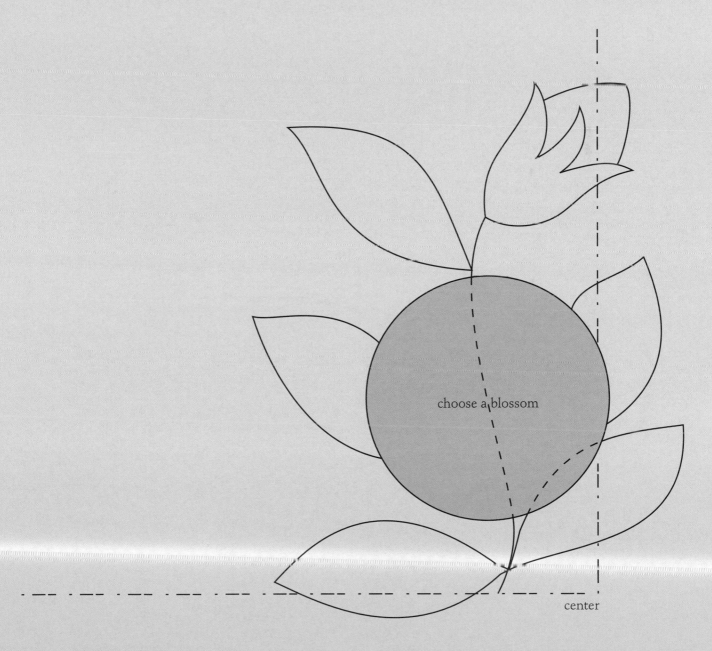

choose a blossom

center

45. MOSS ROSE APPLIQUÉ

This pattern was inspired by a quilt made by Mrs. Susan B. Stayman in 1853. The original design took first prize at the Galesburg, Illinois, Fair in 1855. A winner over 150 years ago, it is still an innovative beauty today This pattern is presented in two sections.

For raw-edge appliqué, cut fabric pieces on the line. For turned edges, add ³⁄₁₆" allowance to fabric pieces.

center

45. MOSS ROSE APPLIQUÉ continued

center

GARDEN IN THE MAZE
52" x 52"

Set and quilted by Ellen Peters, Laconia, NH. Blocks: 1. pattern 22, by the author; 2. pattern 19, by Deborah Fournier-Johnstone, Dover, NH; 3. pattern 36, by the author; 4. pattern 23, by Elizabeth Devlin, Falmouth, MA.

A BED OF ROSES (cover quilt)
47" x 47"

Set and quilted by Ellen Peters, Laconia, NY. Blocks: 1. pattern 23, by Sheila Pearson, Nottingham, England; 2. pattern 4, by the author; 3. pattern 39, by Laura Leigher, Appleton, ME; 4. pattern 37, by Candy Davis, Elkton, MD.

GARDEN VIEW GALLERY

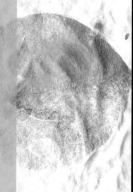

I know a bank whereon the wild thyme blows, where oxslips and nodding violets grow.

Shakespeare,
"A Midsummer's
Nights Dream"

When a gallery quilt contains more than one block, the blocks are numbered left to right, top to bottom.

MY GARDEN QUILT

45" x 45"

Stitched and quilted by Marylou McDonald, Laurel, MD. Marylou included some blocks from other album quilts in this Album quilt. She also created some dimensional fabric blossoms to suit the blocks. Blocks: Row 1. patterns 26, 18, 21, 24; Row 2. pattern 22, available from the author; Row 3. available from the author, 33; Row 4. patterns 30, both patterns available from the author, 23.

THE SECRET GARDEN
32" x 32". Block by Sue Wilson, Cosby, Leicester, England; borders by the author; quilting by Ellen Peters, Laconia, NH. Pattern 12.

JACK FROST IN THE GARDEN
39" x 36". Block by Sue Wilson, Cosby, Leicester, England; borders by the author; quilting by Ellen Peters, Laconia, NH. A simple paper-cut block becomes wonderfully complex when recut and stitched with contrasting fabrics, decorative threads, trims, embroidery, and beadwork. Pattern 12.

COURTYARD URNS
36" x 36". Stitched and quilted by the author. A formal garden would not be complete without urns filled with wonderful flowers. If you love to appliqué, you'll enjoy the challenge of this project. If you want to simplify the block, try fused fabrics with a decorative stitched edge or use gray ultrasuede with an embroidered or couched outline. Pattern 41.

SWEET VIOLETS

56" x 56". *Set and quilted by Ellen Peters, Laconia, NH. A wide violet chintz border provides a sharp contrast with the floral backgrounds of the four blocks. Blocks: 1. pattern 30, by Kate Salt, Derby, England; 2. pattern 40, by Deborah Raver, Fallbrook, CA; 3. pattern 38, by Marylou McDonald, Laurel, MD; 4. pattern 13, by the author.*

ROSE BOUQUET

28" x 28". *Stitched by Gail Rowe, Southboro, MA; flowers by the author; borders and quilting by Ellen Peters, Laconia, NH. This delicate bouquet blooms beautifully on a large-scale floral background fabric. Pattern 44.*

SWIRLING POSIES

26" x 26". *Block by Sue Day, Nottingham, England; border by the author, quilted by Ellen Peters, Laconia, NH. A hand-painted fabric that resembles sky and ground serves as the perfect background for this windblown spray of flowers. Each blossom is cut from chintz and appliquéd to its stem. The border is also a chintz decorator fabric. Pattern 24.*

A SQUARED FRAMED WREATH

24" x 24"

Painted block by Erica Chang, Honolulu, HI; block designed and set by the author; quilted by Ellen Peters, Laconia, NH. A little artistic license was taken with this block. The frame from Pattern 38 sets off the beautiful hand-painted watercolor roses. I had the roses for many years before I found the perfect setting for them in this series. A floral striped border and stippled quilting complete this double-framed floral picture.

SPRING GARDEN

60" x 60"

By Lisa Louise Adams, Volcano, HI. Inspired by the beauty of Hawaiian quilts and album blocks of long ago, Lisa designed this paper-cut wreath. She cut the fabric on the pattern line instead of adding turn-under allowances, so that when she needle-turned the fabric edges, a more delicate design resulted. Cornerstones: 1. pattern 16. 2. pattern 14. 3. pattern 17. 4. pattern 15.

ROSE GARDEN 58" x 58"

Block by Marguerite Shattock, Fresno, CA; quilt set and quilted by Ellen Peters, Laconia, NH. You have to look twice for the flowers in this popular pattern. Embroidered stems, ultra-suede bud calyxes, and ribbon rose buds make quick work of this block. Setting the block on point and surrounding it with decorator fabrics makes this single block grow to a generous lap quilt. Pattern 26.

PANSIES ON MY TABLE

26" x 26", set and quilted by Ellen Peters, Laconia, NH. This one-block runner has its own centerpiece of dimensional ribbon flowers to grace your kitchen table. Pattern 3.

BOTANICAL NOTES

26" x 26", stitched by Donna Downing, Metaire, LA; quilted by the author. A botanical print fabric and a border of vines, roses, and birds gives this block a look of old-world botanical text books. The use of ultrasuede and ruched ribbon makes easy work of this single-flower block. Pattern 40.

GARDEN VIGNETTES

72" x 72", set and bordered by Cheryl Potter, Kingston, NY; quilted by Ellen Peters, Laconia, NH. Novelty prints of sunflowers and garden sheds provide the cornerstone blocks for this theme quilt. Wide green borders make the quilt grow to bed size. Blocks: Row 1. pattern 24, by Judy doBoor, Wichita, KS; Row 2. pattern 1, by Jacque Thompson, Rochester, NH; pattern 31, by Jackie Houldsworth, Portsmouth, NH; pattern 34, by Jan Magee, Denver, CO; Row 3. pattern 33, by the author.

MIDNIGHT GARDEN
50" x 50", set and quilted by Ellen Peters, Laconia, NH. A border fabric of foliage and a wooden trellis provides the theme for this four-block set. Blocks: 1. pattern 12, by the author; 2. pattern 12, by Judith Bentley, Nottingham, England; 3. and 4. patterns 1 and 11, by Corrine Linscott, Holly Hill, FL.

(Blocks are numbered left to right, top to bottom)

HIDDEN GARDEN
51" x 51". Stitched and quilted by Geriann Athans, Plymouth, NH. Geriann created a walled garden quilt inspired by The Secret Garden by Frances Hodgson Burnett. Patterns 1, 5, available from the author, 4.

BIRD IN A GILDED CAGE

26" x 28"

Block by Geriann Athans, Plymouth, NH; borders and quilting by the author. A reproduction fabric creates a border with a design that has a cage-like effect, hence the name of the quilt. Pattern 36

DOWN THE BOULEVARD

60" x 60". Set by Ellen Peters, Laconia, NH. Note the use of buttons as clusters of flowers in this wreath block. The leaves are made from ultrasuede and the stem of decorative trim. Blocks: 1. pattern available from the author, by Paralee Schluchtner, Arvada, CO; 2. and 3. patterns 1 and 2, by the author.

FRIENDSHIP GARDEN MAZE

56" x 68". Blocks by Jennifer Almond, Cosby, England; quilted by Ellen Peters, Laconia, NH. A gift of English chintz fabric was the inspiration for combining four maze patterns into this garden maze quilt. The blocks are machine appliquéd, and the maze quilting in the floral border is stippled. A border of stonework and grass surrounds the floral maze. Patterns 14, 15, 16, 17.

ROSES TO DELIGHT

60" x 60". Block by Barbara Elkhorn, York, ME; borders by the author; quilting by Ellen Peters, Laconia, NH. Wide chintz borders enlarge this one block to a generous-sized wallhanging or lap quilt. Pattern 21.

BIBLIOGRAPHY

SNOWFLAKE II
Stitched by the author. In pairing these floral fabrics, I tried to capture the feel of a lovely garden viewed close up and from afar. Contrasting fabrics were added under the appliqué openings, accented with embroidery stitches. Pattern 3.

Allen, Gloria Seaman, and Nancy Gibson Tuckhorn. *A Maryland Album*. Nashville, Tennessee: Rutledge Hill Press, 1995.

Binney, Edwin, and Gail Binney-Winslow. *Homage to Amanda*. San Francisco: R K Press, 1984.

Bowman, Doris M. *The Smithsonian Treasury of American Quilts*. Washington, D.C.: Smithsonian Institution Press, 1991.

Brackman, Barbara. *Encyclopedia of Appliqué*. McLean, Virginia: EPM Publications, Inc., 1993.

Bullard, Lacy Folmar, and Betty Jo Shiell. *Chintz Quilts: Unfading Glory*. Tallahassee, Florida: Serendipity Publishers, 1983.

Clark, Ricky. *Quilted Gardens – Floral Quilts of the Nineteenth Century*. Nashville, Tennessee: Rutledge Hill Press, 1994.

Cory, Pepper, and Susan McKelvey. *The Signature Quilt*. Saddle Brook, New Jersey: Quilt House Publishing, 1995.

Cross, Mary Bywater. *Treasures in the Trunk*. Nashville, Tennessee: Rutledge Hill Press, 1993.

Finley, Ruth E. *Old Patchwork Quilts and the Women Who Made Them*. McLean, Virginia: EPM Publications, 1992.

Goldsborough, Jennifer Faulds. *Lavish Legacies*. Laurel, Maryland: S&S Graphics, 1994.

Haders, Phyllis. *The Warner Collector's Guide to American Quilts*. New York: Warner Books, Inc., 1981.

Hall, Carrie A., and Rose G. Kretsinger. *The Romance of the Patchwork Quilt*. Mineola, New York: Dover Publications, Inc., 1988.

Havig, Bettina. *Carrie Hall Blocks*. Paducah, Kentucky: American Quilter's Society, 1999.

Katzenberg, Dena S. *Baltimore Album Quilts*. Baltimore: The Baltimore Museum of Art, 1980.

Khin, Yvonne M. *The Collector's Dictionary of Quilt Names & Patterns*. Washington, D.C.: Acropolis Books, Ltd., 1980.

Kimball, Jeana. *Red and Green: An Appliqué Tradition*. Bothell, Washington: That Patchwork Place, 1990.

——. *Reflections of Baltimore*. Bothell, Washington: That Patchwork Place, 1989.

Kolter, Jane Bentley. *Forget Me Not*. New York: Sterling Publishing Co., 1985.

Rehmel, Judy. *The Quilt I.D. Book*. New York: Prentice-Hall Press, 1986.

Sienkiewicz, Elly. *Baltimore Album Quilts: Historic Notes & Antique Patterns*. Lafayette, California: C&T Publishing, 1990.

——. *Baltimore Beauties & Beyond, Vol. I*. Lafayette, California: C&T Publishing, 1989.

——. *Baltimore Beauties & Beyond, Vol. II*. Lafayette, California: C&T Publishing, 1991.

MOSS ROSE APPLIQUÉ

Stitched by Betty Day, Silver Springs, MD. This single rose makes an elegant block. Pattern 45.

SWIRLING POISES

Stitched by Elizabeth Devlin, Falmouth, MA. Silk ribbon embroidered stems and ruched blossoms give this block a realistic look. You can almost smell these flowers. Pattern 24.

SOURCES

Just for one's health... it is very necessary to work in the garden and to see the flowers growing.

Vincent van Gogh

Fabrics
SKYDYES
P.O. Box 370116
West Hartford, CT 06117
Hand painted cottons and silks
www.skydyes.com

Beads
TWE / BEADS
P.O. Box 55
Hamburg, NJ 07419-0055
www.twebeads.com

Ribbons, trims
Flower Garden Ribbons
80 Mt. Vernon Street
Dover, NH 03820

Custom machine quilting
Ellen Peters
27 Tremont Street
Laconia, NH 03820

Teachers
Faye Labanaris
80 Mt. Vernon Street
Dover, NH 03820
Ph: 603-742-0211
Fax: 603-740-9199
e-mail: fayequilt@mediaone.net
workshops, lectures, classes

Ellen Peters
27 Tremont Street
Laconia, NH 03246
Ph: 603-524-6956
Fax: 603-524-7282
e-mail: ebpeters@lr.net
workshops, lectures, classes
custom quilting

Mickey Lawler
P.O. Box 370116
West Hartford, CT 06117
Hand painted cottons and silks
www.skydyes.com
workshops, lectures, classes

ABOUT
THE AUTHOR

MRS. KRETSINGER'S ROSE

Stitched by Mitzie Horne, Rochester, NH. Ultrasuede bud calyxes filled with folded-silk rose buds add dimension to this block. The edges of each appliqué layer are outlined in metallic thread embroidery. Pattern 39.

Faye Labanaris specializes in hand appliqué, including Baltimore Album-style and Hawaiian quilts, ribbon work, and dimensional flowers made with fabric or French wire-edged ribbon. She enjoys teaching and eagerly shares her knowledge with her students. She offers classes to all levels of quilters, inspiring beginners as well as challenging advanced quilters. She has taught in Hawaii and throughout the United States and Great Britain and has written two books, *Blossoms by the Sea: Making Ribbon Flowers for Quilts* and *Quilts With A View*, both published by the American Quilter's Society. Formerly, she was a high-school biology teacher and a science consultant for Dover, New Hampshire, elementary schools. Her husband and two sons have been very supportive of her endeavors.

In 1994, the author was voted National Honored Teacher by her students nationwide in C&T Publishing's first Baltimore Album Revival contest. Her quilt, A Tribute to Celia Thaxter, placed first in its category. Her quilt An English Cottage Garden won third place in the innovative category in the 1998 Second Baltimore Revival contest. She has twice been a state winner in the Great American Quilt Festival, sponsored by the Museum of American Folk Art, and her work has been included in several of Elly Sienkiewicz's Baltimore Beauties and Beyond series.

Faye is a co-producer of "Quilt Hawaii," a quilt show and conference held each year in July on a different Hawaiian island. She also co-produces Quilt Ventures Tours with trips to England, Scotland, New England, and the Northeast.

ROSE TREE I

Stitched by Laura Leigher, Appleton, ME. Bright fabric blossoms and a plaid bias-cut stem make this traditional rose tree stand out against a background of a field of wild flowers and dragonflies. Pattern 42.

OTHER AQS BOOKS

This is only a small selection of the books available from the American Quilter's Society. AQS books are known worldwide for timely topics, clear writing, beautiful color photos, and accurate illustrations and patterns. The following books are available from your local bookseller, quilt shop, or public library.

#6000   US$24.95

#5706   US$18.95

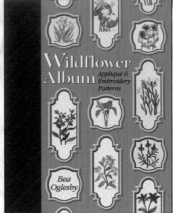

#5757   US$19.95

#6009   US$19.95

#5106   US$16.95

#5234   US$22.95

#6004   US$22.95

#5760   US$18.95

#5848   US$19.95